Paddle Steamer Kingswear Castle

AND STEAMERS OF THE RIVER DART

Richard Clammer & Alan Kittridge

TWELVEHEADS PRESS

TRURO   2013

RICHARD DE JONG

TWELVEHEADS PRESS

First published 2013 by Twelveheads Press
ISBN 978 0 906294 77 2
British Library Cataloguing-in-Publication Data.
A catalogue record for this book is available from the British Library.
Typeset in Frutiger
Printed by Tower Print Ltd., South Wales

All pictures by the authors or from their collections unless otherwise credited.

CONTENTS

The crew of *Berry Castle* of 1880 at Totnes c.1890

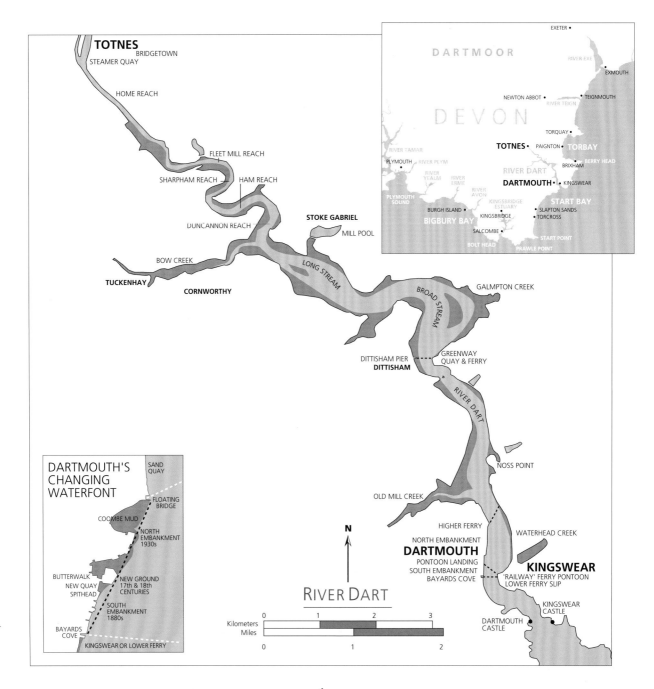

TOTNES
BRIDGETOWN
STEAMER QUAY
HOME REACH
FLEET MILL REACH
SHARPHAM REACH — HAM REACH
DUNCANNON REACH
BOW CREEK
TUCKENHAY   **CORNWORTHY**
STOKE GABRIEL
MILL POOL
LONG STREAM
BROAD STREAM
GALMPTON CREEK
DITTISHAM PIER
DITTISHAM
GREENWAY QUAY & FERRY
RIVER DART
NOSS POINT
OLD MILL CREEK
HIGHER FERRY
WATERHEAD CREEK
NORTH EMBANKMENT
DARTMOUTH
PONTOON LANDING
SOUTH EMBANKMENT
BAYARDS COVE
KINGSWEAR
'RAILWAY' FERRY PONTOON
LOWER FERRY SLIP
KINGSWEAR CASTLE
DARTMOUTH CASTLE

Inset (top right):
D A R T M O O R
EXETER
RIVER EXE
EXMOUTH
NEWTON ABBOT   TEIGNMOUTH
RIVER TEIGN
D E V O N
TORQUAY
RIVER TAMAR
TOTNES PAIGNTON **TORBAY**
PLYMOUTH RIVER PLYM
RIVER DART
BRIXHAM BERRY HEAD
RIVER YEALM
RIVER ERME
DARTMOUTH KINGSWEAR
RIVER AVON
PLYMOUTH SOUND
KINGSBRIDGE ESTUARY
START BAY
BURGH ISLAND
KINGSBRIDGE
SLAPTON SANDS
TORCROSS
BIGBURY BAY
SALCOMBE
START POINT
BOLT HEAD
PRAWLE POINT

Inset (bottom left):
DARTMOUTH'S CHANGING WATERFONT
SAND QUAY
FLOATING BRIDGE
COOMBE MUD
NORTH EMBANKMENT 1930s
BUTTERWALK
NEW QUAY
SPITHEAD
NEW GROUND 17th & 18th CENTURIES
SOUTH EMBANKMENT 1880s
BAYARDS COVE
KINGSWEAR OR LOWER FERRY

N

RIVER DART

Kilometers   0   1   2   3
Miles   0   1   2

4

Where the coast of Devon sweeps into Start Bay, between Berry Head and Start Point, lies the Port of Dartmouth, at the the mouth of river Dart. Rising nearly fifty miles from the sea on Dartmoor the East Dart and West Dart rivers converge at Dartmeet as the river Dart. From the South Hams town of Totnes the final eleven miles of tidal river and estuary (a ria or drowned river valley) are navigable to sea going vessels.

Before the arrival of the railways in the mid-1800s, Dartmouth was relatively isolated, lying well to the south of the main turnpike roads and suffering from the widespread contemporary problem of poor land communications. A high proportion of the area's trade was carried by sea and moved into the hinterland by packhorses, carters' waggons or, whenever possible, by boats along the river, which provided a smoother, faster and more capacious passage for both passengers and cargo. The regional centre of Totnes grew at the head of navigation and prospered in the dual role of market town and river port.

Down the years the Dart has supported a fleet of passenger steamers, the history of which serves to illuminate the sequence of economic and social development through which they passed during the nineteenth and twentieth centuries.

Further afield, the introduction of Europe's first regular, commercially-successful passenger steamboat service by Henry Bell's *Comet* on the Clyde in 1812, was followed by a national boom in the growth of river steamer services. Within two years, the Thames, Tyne, Trent and Tay all boasted steamships, but the innovation took a little longer to reach the more distant and rural Westcountry, and it was not until 1836 that the river Dart greeted its first estuarine passenger steamer. Many of the earliest steamers were jointly owned by large numbers of small shareholders, often local tradesmen whose primary aim was to benefit their existing business interests by improving transport links, but as steamship owning became a viable profit-making activity in its own right there was a noticeable trend towards fewer and therefore larger shareholders. These cargo and passenger services prospered until the coming of the railways forced changes in the patterns of operation.

Faced with railway competition the river steamers increased their dependence on revenue generated by maintaining connecting services for the onward carriage of passengers, mails and cargo brought by train. The railways were also responsible for opening up the Dart estuary to day trippers and thus for generating the excursion trade which, in later years, became the *raison d'etre* for the river steamers' continued existence. The gradual improvement of the road system brought increased competition from lorries and buses and led to further erosion of the steamers' traditional ferry role, until the year-round services were withdrawn and their operators fell back upon excursion sailings as their principal source of income.

The Dart steamers are also worthy of note because of their distinctive design features. The pioneer river steamers of the 1830s had no specifically regional characteristics for many were nomadic and had been built elsewhere, but as the services became established local designs emerged in much the same way as they had with local beach boats and coastal sailing craft. Westcountry shipyards like Harvey of Hayle, Cox & Co. of Falmouth and Philips of Dartmouth refined successive Dart steamers to suit evolving conditions and trade until the ultimate Dart paddle steamer, the *Kingswear Castle* of 1924, reflected her operating environment completely.

We are fortunate indeed that the *Kingswear Castle*, has survived. Lovingly restored to full passenger-carrying condition by the Paddle Steamer Preservation Society, she is the last example of a classic British river paddle steamer in existence and, as such, represents a priceless part of our maritime heritage. She is a beautiful and fascinating vessel in her own right but her historical value is increased many-fold when she is placed in her historical context. It is hoped that, in addition to recording a small piece of our regional maritime history, this book will provide that context, and thus increase the support and enthusiasm of the general public for the continued operational survival of the *Kingswear Castle*.

The accessibility of Dittisham Pier at all states of the tide is illustrated in this picture of *Kingswear Castle* departing and heading upstream during the late 1920s or early 1930s. The hulk of her predecessor lies at the pier prior to being towed upstream and beached at Fleet Mill.

1

VICTORIAN AND EDWARDIAN STEAMBOATS ON THE DART

Navigation

Prior to the construction of a stone weir just north of Totnes in 1581, built to feed water to Totnes town mill, the tidal waters of the Dart estuary reached inland as far as Dartington. However, a thirteenth century stone bridge, a fifteenth century packhorse bridge and, since 1828, the present road bridge, have successively restricted navigation of all but the smallest craft to the tidal reaches of the river immediately downstream from Totnes Bridge.

Since at least the twelfth century, slates had been exported from the quays at Totnes, and between the fifteenth and nineteenth centuries trading vessels from the Continent and London had loaded tin, cloth, wool, leather, granite and cider. The larger barquentines and brigantines of the early nineteenth century, drawing too much water to reach Totnes, had to lay at anchor in Sharpham Reach attended by a fleet of lighters - some 47 in number by the 1830s. In his efforts to reduce the tidal limitations at Totnes, the Duke of Somerset - Edward Augustus Seymour of Berry Pomeroy Castle, embanked about a mile of the riverbank on the Bridgetown (east) bank of the river, below Totnes Bridge. At Bridgetown itself he constructed the quays and warehouses that survived until demolished for car parking in recent years. The Duke also took the lead in setting up, by an Act of Parliament in 1834, the River Dart Navigation Commission, for the purpose of improving the river's navigation by widening and deepening the channel between Totnes Bridge and Langham Wood Point at the mouth of Bow Creek, so that eight feet depth was available at highwater average neap tides (the lowest high tide).

In anticipation of completion of the dredging, a meeting was held at Dartmouth to promote the idea of a steamer communication between the two towns. The *Exeter Flying Post* for 14 January 1836 reports:

> *At a meeting of the inhabitants of Dartmouth, the establishment of a steamboat in the River Dart, with a view to a safe and desirable communication with Totnes, and also for making a means for towing vessels in or out of the harbour, was proposed by Mr. Bill Phillips, and there is an expectation that the plan will be realised.*

Passage boats

During the early years of the nineteenth century, passenger communications were still undertaken by the Dart's passage-boats, which made use of both tide and wind to convey travellers between Dartmouth, Totnes and other intermediate villages and points on the river. An engraving of Totnes Bridge c.1830 portrays a passage-boat anchored off Bridgetown Quay. She is a lug or gaff rigged ketch of about 35-40 feet. Her mainsail bears the names of DARTMOUTH and TOTNES. Passengers are depicted embarking a small rowboat tender together with their luggage, while a second tender awaits offshore. *Murray's Handbook for Devon and Cornwall* (1859) describes an earlier journey aboard the passage-boat:

> *Another excursion from Totnes on a different element, is a trip down the river to Dartmouth. Passage-boats, fare 1s., leave Totnes every tide at high water, and Dartmouth at low water, but, if possible, you should make the voyage towards the close of the day, when lights and shadows are boldly grouped by a declining sun.*

The handbook notes the Dartmouth landing place as being '... *upon the Island of New Ground, which was reclaimed from the river about a century ago.*' This area lies near the present day pontoon landing, adjacent to the tidal basin of the Boat Float. New Ground was embanked for the first time in 1684 and a small stone bridge or causeway built to link it with the Butterwalk. Although this quay was extended in 1740, another 140 years were to elapse before the South Embankment was constructed. The first generation of Dart passenger steamers were therefore restricted to the limited facilities offered by New Ground quay.

Early river steamers

The first recorded river steamer to appear on the Dart was noted in the diary of John Webber Chaster of Totnes:

> Saturday 18th June 1836. For about 3 weeks there has been a Steamer plying on the River twice a day from Dartmouth the property of a Company in the provision of a regular steam communication from London which has been established in the last three months in consequence of the deepening of the River Dart. The river steamer a vessel of about 30 tons is called the Paul Pry she is in a shattered state and they talk of building a new one if it is found to answer which I think it will as it already appears to supersede the passage boats, for surely one would rather be walking the deck of a steamer than be cooped up with Tinkers, Chimney Sweeps and Organ Grinders in a working tub.

While we may all concur with his final sentiment, John Webber Chaster unfortunately fails to satisfy regarding the identity of the operating 'Company'. Paul Pry was built in Hereford in 1827 by William Radford, she measured 31 tons, was registered in Chepstow, and owned by the Wye Steam Packet Company. Following a short but nomadic career on the Mersey and in north Wales she was sold to the St George Steam Packet Company in 1832 and, although her registry was closed in 1835 'vessel lost date unknown', she turned up on the Dart in 1836, probably running a linking service between Dartmouth and Totnes in connection with coastal packets.

A later contributor to the Dartmouth Chronicle in 1895 recalled:

> Dartmothians then bought an old tub called the Paul Pry of 1823 [sic] - Capt Lamble, which ran up and down the River Dart on the Bridgetown side taking two hours for the trip. The Dart [see below], a fine boat, took one and a half hours for the trip and worked on the Totnes side. There was furious competition for some time.

The Dart mentioned above was built by Andrew Bell of North Shields in 1836 and first registered at Dartmouth in May 1837. She was a 66.5 feet long, three masted, lugger rigged, paddle steamer. All 64 of her shares were owned by the Dart Steam Navigation Company (D.S.N.Co.), the trustees of which were: Arthur Howe Holdsworth of Brixham, local landowner, Governor of Dartmouth Castle and once MP for Dartmouth; Thomas Fogwill, a Dartmouth shipowner; and Thomas Shore, Cornfactor of Totnes. She was placed under the management of R. L. Hingston & Sons, Shipping Agents and Merchants of Dartmouth, and advertised as 'The Dart Steamer, conveying goods and passengers to and from Totnes every day'. In the following year, on 28 May, George Hingston bought her from the D.S.N.Co., but found her operation uneconomic and within three years offered her for sale once again. His advertisement in the Exeter Flying Post, 28 May 1840 read:

> Steamer for sale - to be sold by public auction at the Castle Hotel on Friday 5th June at 2 o'clock in the afternoon. THE DART STEAMER - with all her materials, was built in North Shields in 1836. Length 66.5 ft., Beam 14.2 ft., Depth 8.2 ft., $17\frac{1}{2}$ tons, draws four feet of water. She has been employed in River Navigation and in towing shipping in and out of this harbour, is a most desirable vessel and in a perfect state. For viewing and further particulars apply to Messrs Hingston & Sons, Merchants, Dartmouth.

In the event she was not sold until 23 June of the following year when 16 shares each were sold to Capt. John Bulley, Daniel Codner, Robert Harris and Henry Petherbridge, all of Dartmouth. Her brief career on the river Dart drew to a close six months later when she was sold off the river to the Truro & Falmouth Steam Packet Company. The Paul Pry had departed previously.

During the following fourteen years two London built paddle steamers were to ply upon the river, although there is

The *Dartmouth Castle* of 1885 steams down Home Reach, with Totnes behind. This stretch of the river was embanked and improved for navigation by the River Dart Navigation Commission in the 1830s.

an element of doubt concerning their actual periods of operation. The 73 ft. wooden paddler *Violante* was built at Limehouse in 1839 and was lugger rigged with a single mast, bowsprit and woman's bust figurehead. However she was not registered at Dartmouth until 1847, at which time her owners included John Reed Fogwill, a coal merchant of Totnes who owned many of the river's lighters and was also collector of the River Dart Navigation Commission's tolls. Samuel and Henry Follet, Shipbuilders and Shipowners of Dartmouth, also held 16 shares. The Follets maintained a goods and passenger sailing packet run between Hay's Wharf in London and south Devon ports. Thomas Mortimore was her master.

The second steamer was the *Undine*, an 89.5 ft. iron paddler built by Thames Ironworks in 1847. She was possibly purchased in anticipation of the increased trade promised by the imminent arrival of the South Devon Railway in Totnes. *Undine* was owned by John Campbell, Capt. John Bulley (briefly a shareholder of the *Dart* in 1841), and others. A collision report in the *Exeter Flying Post*, 16 December 1852, provides a rare reference to her otherwise quiet but seemingly successful career on the river:

> The UNDINE *steamer, on her passage from Totnes to Dartmouth ran into an empty lighter that was coming up river, belonging to Mr. John Fogwill* [shareholder of the opposing

THE ROYAL STEAMBOAT

DARTMOUTH

Will ply from June 18 to June 30, as follows :
(Circumstances permitting.)

Taking Passengers for Greenway, Dittisham, and Duncannon.

JUNE.	FROM DARTMOUTH.		FROM TOTNES.	
	a.m.	p.m.	a.m.	p.m.
18 Monday ...	6 15	1 4	8 35	2 30 6 15
19 Tuesday ...	6 15	2	9	6 15
20 Wednesday	6 15	3 30	9	6 15
21 Thursday ...	6 15 9 30	3 30	8 11	6 15
22 Friday	6 15 9 30	4	8 11 30	6 15
23 Saturday ...	6 15 9 30	4 15	8 11 30	6 15
25 Monday ...	6 15 9 30	1 15	8 11 15	6 30
26 Tuesday ...	7 9 30	1 30	8 30 11 30	3 15
27 Wednesday	7	2	9	4 15
28 Thursday ...	9	3 30	11 30	4 30
29 Friday	9 30	3 30	11 30	5 30
30 Saturday ...	6	3 30	11 30	6 15

FARES :—Main Cabin and Ladies' Saloon, 1s. 3d., Return Tickets, 2s. ; Fore Cabin, 9d., Return Tickets, 1s. 3d.

The "Dartmouth" was built by Scott, Russell & Co. expressly to suit the requirements of the River, combining from her peculiar construction, speed, stability, and public accommodation.

A Copy of the Monthly Time Tables and Season Tickets may be obtained of Mr. Fogwill, Totnes, or Mr. Mortimore, Managing Owner, Dartmouth.

Violante]. The lighter sunk and one poor fellow - Giles Shinner was drowned - it was dark at the time. There was great blame to the captain for not carrying lights after being cautioned so many times. It is to be hoped the owners will see into this.

The old passage-boats that had once conveyed travellers to the stage coach at Totnes, gradually faded away, while the *Undine* and *Violante* prospered from the arrival of the railway at Totnes on 20 July 1848. After *Violante* was broken up in 1854, the *Undine* enjoyed a two year monopoly of steamer services on the river, until in 1856 two new contenders entered the competition for the river's passenger trade.

Origins of the River Dart Steamboat Co.Ltd.

When Charles Seale Hayne, nephew of the Baronet - Sir Henry Seale of Mount Boone, inherited his father's fortune in 1854, he lost little time in furthering his ambitions in local business ventures. Foremost amongst his early schemes was the promotion of the Dartmouth & Torbay Railway Company and the creation of a steam packet company to serve its planned Kingswear terminus, and also to compete against the allegedly unreliable *Undine* for the Totnes traffic. The Dartmouth & Torbay Railway Company was incorporated in 1857 to extend the South Devon Railway Company's Torquay branch to a terminus at Hoodown near Kingswear (extended into Kingswear in 1863), linked to Dartmouth by ferry.

Meanwhile, on 22 August 1856, at Deptford Green Dock in London, the 90.2 ft. paddle steamer *Louisa* was launched. Her major shareholder was a Yorkshire shipowner, John Moody of Goole, who held 48 shares. Seale Hayne, who owned the balance of 16 shares, prepared her for use on the Dartmouth - Totnes steamer service.

Another paddler had been launched in London just fifteen days earlier. Built by John Scott Russell at Millwall, the 85.3 ft. iron paddle steamer *Dartmouth* was also destined for the river Dart passenger trade. Her owners were: Robert Moisey Mortimore, watchmaker; Arthur Howe Holdsworth – the Seale family's arch political and commercial rival; Henry Petherbridge; and Walter Septimus Reed, all of Dartmouth. So close was the race to complete and operate the steamers on the Dart, that they not only carried consecutive official numbers - *Dartmouth* 17881/*Louisa* 17882 - but also had consecutive Dartmouth Port numbers - 27 and 28 respectively.

However, the *Dartmouth* stole a march on *Louisa* in being ready for the Royal Family's visit to Dartmouth in August 1856, on board the Royal Yacht. Subsequent advertisements and reports in the *Totnes Weekly Times* refer to the 'Royal Steamboat Dartmouth' or the 'Royal Dartmouth'. Although never officially renamed, *Dartmouth* adopted her 'Royal' appendage during the Royal visit, when she conveyed the Royal visitors on the river Dart, to view Totnes.

Pilot moored off Kingswear c.1860s. COURTESY DARTMOUTH MUSEUM

On 6 October 1856 Moody and Seale Hayne's *Louisa* ran her maiden trip on the river Dart. She was joined in the same month by a running partner, Moody's 95 ft. iron paddler *Mary*, transferred from the north east to help maintain a two steamer opposition against *Undine* and *Dartmouth*. Seale Hayne bought 16 shares in *Mary* and in 1858 bought 32 shares in Moody's 84.8 ft. iron paddler *Pilot* (ex-*British Hero*), which was transferred from South Shields to engage in the towage trade in Dartmouth Harbour. In the same year *Dartmouth*'s owners reportedly rejected a profitable offer from her builder, John Scott Russell, to buy her back on behalf of the Government for David Livingstone's imminent Zambezi expedition.

Dartmouth Steam Packet Co. Ltd.

On 19 March 1859 both Moody and Seale Hayne sold their shares in *Louisa* to Seale Hayne's newly incorporated Dartmouth Steam Packet Co. Ltd. (D.S.P.Co.Ltd), the directors of which also included Henry Carew Hunt, and Charles Vincent as Company Secretary. W. H. Rees was appointed Manager. In August of the same year the D.S.P.Co.Ltd. acquired 40 shares and, therefore, controlling interest in the *Pilot*. The *Mary* and John Moody returned to the north of England.

Louisa had a complete refit at '*Kelly's Patent Slip*' at Sandquay, Dartmouth in 1860. This yard had been taken over by Kelly's ex-foreman shipbuilder, George Philip in 1858, laying the foundation of Philip & Son Ltd. The paddle tug *Pilot* provided an extended coastal trip to Weymouth in July 1859, carrying 50 excursionists from Dartmouth, Torquay, Teignmouth and other Devonshire towns. She left Weymouth the next morning for the return voyage. During the following winter she went to Plymouth, to be refitted and surveyed as a full time coastal excursion boat. She performed her first trip in this capacity on 28 May 1860, departing from New Ground at 10am and visiting Torquay. On subsequent Torquay excursions she offered trips from Torquay to Slapton Sands. During this first season *Pilot* provided some Channel Island trips and also operated some inter-island runs between Guernsey and Herm.

On the 14 March 1861 the Dartmouth & Torbay Railway was opened through to Brixham Road (now Churston) Station. It was to be a further three years before the line eventually tunnelled through Greenway to reach Kingswear. In the interim the Dart steamers, which had already been making some calls at Greenway, Dittisham and Duncannon, included Greenway Quay as a regular call on every trip in each direction. For three years a horse drawn omnibus linked Brixham Road Station to Greenway Quay, and regular timetables were adhered to, corresponding with train times. For example, the 6.00am boat from Dartmouth met the 6.45 omnibus to

A rare view of a pre-1880 river Dart paddle steamer, moored at St Peter's Quay, Totnes c.1860. She might be either *Dartmouth* or *Newcomin*, both of which possessed features corresponding to those seen in this picture. As the Dartmouth Steam Packet Co. Ltd's Newcomin used Steamer Quay on the opposite side of the river, this could indicate the steamer's identity as the rival *Dartmouth*. TOTNES MUSEUM SOCIETY

connect with the 7.20 train at Brixham Road. Four Dartmouth - Greenway runs were provided daily. The fare was 4d. in the fore cabin and 6d. in the after cabin. From Totnes the fare to Greenway was 6d. and 1s. respectively.

A single Dartmouth-Totnes ticket for *Louisa*'s cabin cost 1s., return 1s.6d. The main cabin was 1s.6d. and 2s.6d. respectively. Departure times depended upon the tides, but she offered three trips each way whenever possible, sometimes leaving Totnes as early as 6.00am. There were no Sunday services.

Perhaps in the knowledge that the D.S.P.Co.Ltd. were building a new steamer (see below), Robert Mortimore, who between 1858-1862 had acquired all *Dartmouth*'s shares, seemingly 'threw in the towel' and sold his steamer to William Froude of Paignton for £1,020. Froude, a civil engineer and son-in-law of Arthur Howe Holdsworth (who died in 1860), was also a business associate of Seale Hayne and a fellow Director of the Dartmouth & Torbay Railway. Froude pioneered research in fluid dynamics on hull shapes, in which capacity he had assisted I. K. Brunel and the Royal Navy. It is possible the wealthy Froude used *Dartmouth* during his experiments in Dartmouth Harbour.

The long awaited opening of the Dartmouth & Torbay Railway through to its Kingswear terminus was imminent in June 1864, when the D.S.P.Co.Ltd.'s new 108 ft. iron paddler *Newcomin* arrived. A description of the steamer and of her trial trip to Totnes on Friday 1 July 1864, appeared in the *Western Daily Mercury*:

> The new river steamboat NEWCOMIN made her trial trip on Friday afternoon last. Invitation tickets were sent out to about 140 persons for the trip, but the number who went were at least 160. At 19 minutes to 5 amid the hearty cheers of those on shore, answered by the still heartier ones of those on board, the NEWCOMIN started for her first trip up the 'English Rhine'. At starting, forty revolutions per minute were obtained, which increased to fifty when off Dittisham, which place was reached in eighteen minutes. Stoke Gabriel was reached in 31 minutes. At the sight of the new steamer with her living freight, wending her circuitous route by that most beautiful part of the river, Sharpham

> Woods, old men from their boats waved their hats, and happy hay making parties from the adjoining fields cheered the new comer, as she steered steadily onward. At 17 minutes to 6 the boat was alongside Totnes Quay, the entire distance being done in one hour and two minutes, against a strong wind and tide. On landing at Totnes the greater portion of the excursionists adjourned to the Seymour Hotel, where the toasts of 'success to the NEWCOMIN', 'The Directors' and 'the Totnes shareholders' were proposed and appropriately responded to. The return trip was run in exactly one hour. The NEWCOMIN was built by Messrs Lewis & Stockwell of London and is 108 ft. long and 12 ft. beam, and her engines are 20 horse power, by Messrs James Watt & Co. Her paddle boxes are to be enlarged, which it is expected will make a difference of a mile and a half an hour in her speed, the builders seeing the improvement necessary.

The Dartmouth & Torbay Railway finally opened throughout on 16 August 1864, worked by the South Devon Railway Company. It should come as no surprise that under Seale Hayne's chairmanship, the Dartmouth & Torbay Railway Company leased the Kingswear - Dartmouth ferry operation to his Dartmouth Steam Packet Co. Ltd. The railway company acquired a double ended paddle steamer, the *Perseverance*, for the Dartmouth Steam Packet Co. Ltd. to run the ferry with. She was prepared for service by Lewis & Stockwell of London but for the next six years the appropriately named steamer severely tested everybody's patience being far more costly than anticipated, difficult to handle and mechanically unreliable. To maintain their river link between Dartmouth and Kingswear Station at all states of the tide, the Dartmouth & Torbay Railway Company constructed pontoon landings on both banks of the river, for the use of the ferry lessees only. In addition, Dartmouth Station was built at the entrance to Dartmouth pontoon, to issue railway tickets which included the cost of the ferry passage. Railway travellers could now choose Kingswear or Totnes as their railway station, but either way their journey required the services of D.S.P.Co.Ltd. operated steamers.

The *Undine* at this time required an extensive overhaul and

The *Eclair* at Ilfracombe during her time in the Bristol Channel between 1869 to 1872.

was sold off the river to Waterford owners in 1864. Some documents suggest that serious faults were found and she was broken up, while others report that she was subsequently in use as a ferry boat on the river Suir at Waterford.

The arrival of the railway at Kingswear revived Seale Hayne's interest in Channel Island steamer services, which had previously been operated by *Pilot*, and in June 1865 the D.S.P.Co.Ltd. took delivery of the 179.8ft., sea-going, iron paddler, *Eclair*. She gained a Class 3 sea going excursion certificate for 299 persons, and a Class 2 home trade certificate (to permit Channel crossings) for 237. In *Westcountry Passenger Steamers*, Graham Farr recorded her basic programme: Departing from Dartmouth on a Monday night, she arrived in Guernsey, Jersey and St. Malo the following day. On Wednesday she left St. Malo, called at Jersey and Guernsey arriving at Plymouth on Thursday. She departed from Plymouth the next day and called into Dartmouth, Guernsey and Jersey only, returning to Dartmouth on Saturday. She followed a similar pattern of sailings between May and October during 1866 and 1867, but the service was unsuccessful. In 1868 she was laid up and sold in October for future use in the Bristol Channel and later on the Thames and south east coast.

The *Western Daily Mercury* for 21 February 1866 reported yet another refit for *Louisa*:

> The LOUISA, steamboat, well known on the River Dart, having recently undergone some considerable repairs and alterations, made a trial trip to this town (Totnes) from Dartmouth on Saturday (14 February 1866), with a number of passengers. We are informed that the speed of this boat although previously very good, is now increased, and that she still bids fair to retain her character of being the fastest boat on the Dart.

But the *Louisa*'s seemingly successful time on the river ended two years later in 1868 when, although only 12 years old, she was inexplicably broken up - although two big refits in eight years suggest some problem. Her reputation as the Dart's premier passenger steamer was inherited by *Newcomin*. The *Totnes Times & Gazette* for June 1868 notes: '*The fast steamboat NEWCOMIN plies between Totnes and Dartmouth daily*'. *Pilot* was the D.S.P.Co.Ltd.'s only other operational steamer in 1868, the company had acquired all of her shares by 1866.

Two new paddlers were built by Harvey's of Hayle in 1869. The *Dolphin* was a 104.6ft., iron hulled steamer, the

Dolphin at the railway ferry pontoon, Kingswear. Owned by the successive railway companies she was initially operated by the Dartmouth Steam Packet Co.Ltd.

DARTMOUTH.—FROM KINGSWEAR PIER

Dartmouth & Torbay Railway's replacement for the disastrous *Perseverance* of 1863. Similar to the *Perseverance* she was double ended and fitted with rudders fore and aft, to facilitate manoeuvring at the pontoons. She carried 331 passengers and was to maintain the ferry for exactly 40 years. However, the *Perseverance* still had one 'joker' to play, the railway company fitted her re-furbished machinery into the *Dolphin*. But the engine continued to cause trouble and needed replacing within five years, by which time the railway company had taken over operation of the ferry from the D.S.P.Co.Ltd.

The second new steamer in 1869 was the D.S.P.Co.Ltd.'s 100ft. wooden paddle tug *Guide*. She might have been purchased to fill a dual passenger/towage roll, but seems to have been replaced in her passenger duties by the company's next purchase, in 1871, of William Froude's *Dartmouth*. In the next year *Guide* was chartered to run between Penzance and the Isles of Scilly, following the sudden demise of the Scilly Isles Steam Navigation Company after the loss of their screw steamer *Little Western* at Samson Island on 6 October 1872. The charter continued until 1875.

The D.S.P.Co.Ltd.'s fleet in 1876 comprised the *Pilot*, *Newcomin* and *Dartmouth*. The *Guide* had also returned from her Isles of Scilly charter. During the following year a new regime gained ownership of all the river's passenger steamers, establishing an executive that was to remain in control of the river's steamers until 1952.

The Dartmouth & Torbay Steam Packet Company

On 1 February 1876 the Great Western Railway (G.W.R.) took over working the South Devon Railway, including the Dartmouth & Torbay line and the railway ferry between Kingswear and Dartmouth. A year later Seale Hayne's D.S.P.Co.Ltd. bowed out, selling it's fleet of steamers to a new syndicate of local businessmen. Seale Hayne's right hand man in Dartmouth was his solicitor, William Smith and on 15 February 1877 the D.S.P.Co.Ltd. sold Smith 32 shares in the *Dartmouth*. Jasper Bartlett, a Merchant in Brixham, William

Nimble moored in Dartmouth Harbour.

Ball, a Torquay Coal Merchant and William Whiteway of Torquay, each took eight shares. Four shares each went to William Henry Punchard and James Reed Tolman, both described as retired ships masters of Dartmouth. Tolman was appointed as managing owner. *Pilot*, *Newcomin* and *Guide* were similarly sold off to members of the same syndicate, although *Guide* was immediately re-sold to T. & C. Jackson at Milford. The new group also took delivery of a 61.6ft. iron, screw steamer *Hauley*, built by Harvey's of Hayle during the same year. William Smith was the major shareholder of this new boat with 24 shares, 16 of which he soon sold to Thomas Whiteway Eales and William Ball. The other shareholders were Edward Marsh Turnor, Jasper Bartlett, William Whiteway, William Punchard and James Reed Tolman. The group named themselves the Dartmouth & Torbay Steam Packet Company (D.& T.S.P.Co.).

The new D.& T.S.P.Co. were contracted to provide a steamer and crew as a replacement for the *Dolphin* if required at £5 per day, with a minimum guarantee of £150 per annum and access to the pontoon landings. On the 1 August 1878 the South Devon and Dartmouth & Torbay railway companies were dissolved and the lines taken over by the G.W.R.

The *Pilot* was sold in 1879 to George Perkins Ward of Teignmouth and a new 57.8ft. wood, screw steamer, the *Nimble*, purchased. Built at Brixham in 1878, her major

Berry Castle at Steamer Quay, Bridgetown, Totnes, before 1904, flying the 'DTSPC' pennant and wearing the black funnel colour of the Dartmouth & Torbay Steam Packet Company.

P. S. BERRY CASTLE of 1880

shareholders were William Smith and William Ball, but all of the other company members, with one new addition - Mary Mackey, held smaller shareholdings. William Punchard was appointed manager. On 27 July 1880 the company's first major steamer was launched from Polyblank's yard in Waterhead Creek at Kingswear. Berry Castle was a 108ft. iron, paddle steamer, the design of which set the standard for all but one of the Dart's future paddlers. The hull was floated out under the railway embankment and fitted out in Philip's Sanquay yard in Dartmouth. Shares were taken up by all members of the D.& T.S.P.Co., with Ball and Smith once again taking the largest number. J. R. Tolman, with 4 shares, was appointed manager. Berry Castle's arrival signalled the end for the 25

year old Dartmouth. She was broken up in Bristol City Docks and her registry cancelled in 1881.

During the early 1880s the Dartmouth Harbour Commissioners, under the leadership of Charles Seale Hayne, with William Smith as his Secretary, promoted a scheme for embanking the shoreline from Bayards Cove to Spithead (New Ground) near Dartmouth railway station. Overcoming strong opposition, the South Embankment development was completed in 1882, the Boat Float being additionally formed to retain access from the river to New Quay. The Embankment transformed the Dartmouth waterfront and greatly improved the landing facilities for passenger and

Berry Castle in Sharpham Reach

The steam launch *Dart* pictured during her time on the Kingsbridge estuary in the 1890s. COURTESY ROBERT CHAPMAN

other boats. The Embankment extension, north of the railway station, across Coombe Mud to Sandquay was not constructed until 1930.

Another screw steamer was purchased by the D.& T.S.P.Co. in 1883. She was the *Dart*, a 54.4ft. steel vessel built by Gabriel Davis of Abingdon, Berkshire. A typical product of the upper Thames boatbuilders, she looked more like a private steam yacht than a passenger steamer. Her initial owners, J. R.Tolman and W. H. Punchard, owned 32 shares each, but by 25 October of the same year the shares were distributed amongst the all the members of the company. The *Dart* was used on the lightly loaded winter service.

In July 1884 the *Newcomin* was sold to French owners, leaving *Berry Castle* temporarily as the sole Dartmouth-Totnes paddler. However, *Newcomin*'s sale heralded the arrival of a new 100ft. steel paddler, the *Dartmouth Castle*, built by Harvey's & Co. of Hayle in 1885. She was fitted with a 2 cylinder oscillating engine and her speed was given as 10 miles per hour. Tolman and Punchard held 32 shares each, but after

Berry Castle departing from Steamer Quay, Totnes. Her black funnel and 'RDSC' pennant indicate the date as 1904/5, after which a yellow and black funnel colour was adopted.

River Dart, Steamer leaving Totnes.

Dartmouth Castle at Steamer Quay, Totnes. The Dartmouth & Torbay Steam Packet Company 'DTSPC' pennant is flown at her masthead, dating this picture to pre-1904. She possessed a slightly shorter funnel than *Berry Castle*, with the first funnel ring positioned a third the way down from the top. In addition her paddle boxes were fitted with steps on the forward half, while *Berry Castle*'s were on the aft side. COURTESY A. R. KINGDOM

a series of transactions in September 1885 and April 1886, the other members of the D.& T.S.P.Co. had acquired their quotas, leaving messrs Ball and Smith once again as leading shareholders.

There followed almost a decade of stability for the river's passenger steamer fleet. The two paddlers, *Berry Castle* and *Dartmouth Castle*, assisted by the three small screw steamers, *Hauley*, *Nimble* and *Dart*, fulfiled the company's requirements on the river. The *Dolphin* continued alone on the Kingswear Ferry, substituted by one of the D.& T.S.P.Co.'s screw steamers

when required. In May 1893 all of the company's shares in the *Dart* were sold to Nicholas March, shipowner of Salcombe, who used her on the similar Salcombe-Kingsbridge steamer link. Advertisements in the *Totnes Times & Devon News* during 1894 provide a clear picture of the steamers being used on the Dartmouth-Totnes river service for that year. In January the D.& T.S.P.Co. were running *Glenalva*, a 12 seater passenger launch. The advertisement notes that due to lack of space aboard the launch, no special rate market tickets could be issued. From February until September the *Berry Castle* and

A rare view of the flush decked *Totnes Castle* on the Dart, approaching Steamer Quay, Totnes, prior to 1904.

Dartmouth Castle shared the route, providing two trips each way per day. The saloon was 1s. single and the fore cabin 9d. Persons taking excursion tickets were not allowed to carry luggage. In 1896 the two paddlers were joined by the new 79ft. steel *Totnes Castle* built by Philip of Dartmouth. She was a smaller flush decked vessel, introduced, perhaps, to maintain the winter service. Her compound, diagonal, direct acting engines were supplied by Lees Anderson & Co. The major shareholders were William Ball, William Smith and James Reed Tolman, although Tolman later sold all but four of his shares to other members of the company. Both Tolman and Punchard were designated as managing owners.

The iron screw steamer *Hauley* was the next vessel to be sold. Her Dartmouth registry was closed in 1898 when she was sold to Liverpool owners who renamed her *Greenfinch*.

George Clift of Romsdal, Dartmouth, bought into the company in December 1900. James Reed Tolman died on 13 April 1901, and his shareholdings passed jointly to: John Jago Tolman, proprietor of the Dartmouth Ironmongery Stores on

The Quay; Fredrick James Tolman; and David Russell Jacks. Later in the year J. J. Tolman bought the shareholdings of the other two. William Smith died in February 1904 and his executors (sons), Granville Smith, of the Supreme Court, and Hayne Smith, became joint owners of his substantial shareholding. Charles Seale Hayne had died only months before in 1903.

The D.& T.S.P.Co. took delivery of a fourth paddle steamer in 1904. The 107.6ft. steel paddler *Kingswear Castle* was built by Cox & Co. of Falmouth. Her engines, also built by Cox, were surface condensing, compound diagonal.

The River Dart Steamboat Co.Ltd.

Reference to Torbay in the Dartmouth & Torbay Steam Packet Company's title was now considered redundant and following the arrival of *Kingswear Castle* the opportunity was taken to rename the company the River Dart Steamboat Company. Two years later, on 30 May 1906, the legal process of incorporating the company began.

Wearing the new yellow and black funnel colours of the River Dart Steamboat Co. Ltd., *Dartmouth Castle* is moored at South Embankment, Dartmouth.

S.S. "DARTMOUTH CASTLE" LEAVING DARTMOUTH.

Kingswear Castle (1904) steams up Home Reach, approaching Steamer Quay, Totnes, where *Berry Castle* is already moored.

Hayne Smith was engaged as solicitor in the formation of the River Dart Steamboat Co. Ltd. William Ball, John Jago Tolman and George Clift consented to act as directors. Each agreed to take 50 shares of £10 each. The Nominal Capital was to be £15,000 divided into shares of £10 each. The company's objects were:

> *To acquire and take over as a going concern and carry on the business of Ship Owners, Shippers and Excursion Agents now carried on at Dartmouth and Totnes, in the County of Devon, and elsewhere, under the style or firm of the River Dart Steamboat Company (and formerly under the style or firm of the Dartmouth & Torbay Steam Packet Company). .. to acquire as part of the above named, property and assets, by purchase or otherwise, the steamships DARTMOUTH CASTLE, KINGSWEAR CASTLE, TOTNES CASTLE and BERRY CASTLE.*

The subscribers were William Ball, Hayne Smith, Jasper Bartlet, Thomas Whiteway Eales, George Clift, John J. Tolman and Harry Marsh Turnor, each taking one share. The company was incorporated on 9 June 1906 as Company No. 89081. The registered office was on South Embankment. A series of transactions on the same day transferred ownership of the four paddlers to the new company. The total number of shares allocated was 1008, of which none were exchanged for cash.

The steel hulled *Kingswear Castle* of 1904 at Steamer Quay, Totnes.

The *Berry Castle* steaming down Home Reach with Totnes in the background. Just behind is *Kingswear Castle* (1904) approaching the Totnes landing stage.
DEVON LIBRARY SERVICES, LOCAL STUDIES LIBRARY

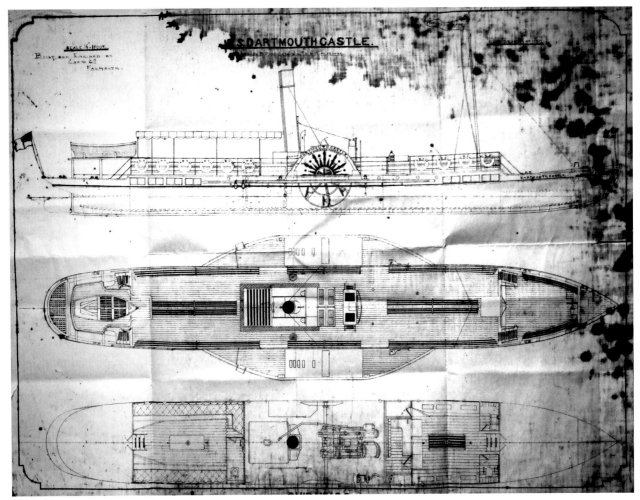

General arrangement diagram of the Cox & Co. of Falmouth built *Dartmouth Castle* of 1907.

Dartmouth Castle of 1885 in Ireland on the river Blackwater at Youghal.

44794. Totnes, Landing Stage.

The second *Dartmouth Castle* of 1907 moored at Steamer Quay. Her appearance was to alter over the years, but pictured here, as built, she was the last of the company's paddlers constructed to a similar general arrangement as BERRY CASTLE. Her deck was later extended out over her sponsons.

They were allotted '*in consideration of the allottees being parties to executing such transfers as might be desired necessary*', (i.e. - in proportion to their shareholdings in the steamers). William Ball received 252 fully paid up £10 shares. Granville Smith and Hayne Smith jointly held 189 shares. Jasper Bartlett received 126, as did Thomas Whiteway Eales. Mary Mackey, George Clift and John J.Tolman held 63 shares each. Harry Marsh Turnor and Richard Arthur Warburton inherited E. Marsh Turnor's 26 shares. George Clift, the Company Secretary, was appointed as Manager.

On 16 November 1906, an Extraordinary General Meeting passed a special resolution authorising the directors to raise £3000 as 60 Debentures of £50 at 5% per annum. The money was used to finance a replacement for *Dartmouth Castle*.

An order was placed with Cox & Co. of Falmouth to construct a new 100ft. steel paddler:

> *To be a light draft steamer similar in general design to the Company's paddle steamer DARTMOUTH CASTLE, with a break deck about 68ft. in length, and cockpits forward and aft of the same, about 21ft. and 11ft, to sternpost in length respectively.*

She was named *Dartmouth Castle*, replacing the original steamer of that name which was sold in June 1907 to new owners on the river Blackwater in Ireland.

Berry Castle (outside) and *Kingswear Castle* (1904) at Steamer Quay, Totnes.

2

DART STEAMERS BETWEEN TWO WARS

In the summer of 1908 the *Great Western Railway Magazine* reported:

> *Passengers who are in the habit of visiting Dartmouth will have noted that the old paddle steamer* DOLPHIN *has recently been removed from service on the Kingswear and Dartmouth Ferry, and that her place has been taken by a new and up-to-date ferry steamer named* THE MEW. *Her replacement severs many old associations and marks the removal of an old and familiar feature on the waters of the Dart.*

Mr. C. Irvine Davidson, the G.W.R. Steamboat Superintendent, was called upon to prepare the design and specification for the new ferry steamer, and the building contract was placed with Cox & Co. of Falmouth. She was a 90.2ft steel, twin-screw vessel, fitted with two sets of inverted, direct-acting, compound engines, giving a speed of 10 knots. The severed '*old associations*' referred back to the Dartmouth & Torbay Railway and the Dartmouth Steam Packet Company Ltd. *The Mew* entered service on 31 May 1908.

The Dartmouth Shipping Register notes that the registry of the screw steamer *Nimble* was closed in 1910 - '*vessel broken up at Dartmouth*'. She doesn't appear to have been included amongst the steamers transferred to the R.D.S.Co.Ltd. in 1906. The *Totnes Castle*'s stay on the river also came to an end in 1912 when her registry was transferred to the Port of Poole on 13 November. A Bill of Sale dated 30 August 1912 transferred ownership to Mabel Constance Alice Biss of Poole. The paddler was renamed *Wareham Queen* and provided excursions in Poole Harbour and from Poole to Wareham on the river Frome.

The Dart's market-day trade was never large enough to support a special steamer, although attempts were made to attract such custom. Reference is made in some earlier steamer advertisements to the issue of 'Market-Tickets', which provided a special rate for market produce. Dittisham and the mouth of Bow Creek were pick-up points for passengers and produce on market and other days. At low tides boatmen rowed out to meet the steamer off Dittisham Quay, whilst passengers and goods from Cornworthy awaited the steamer in small boats, off Bow Creek.

In 1914 the vacancy created by *Totnes Castle*'s sale was filled by a new 108ft. steel paddler named *Compton Castle*.

P. S. COMPTON CASTLE of 1914

Built by Cox & Co., she was the first paddle steamer in the fleet to be constructed with her deck extended onto elongated paddle sponsons, and the first to have portholes instead of square saloon windows.

During the early stages of the Great War, the summer excursions continued, virtually unabated but later a reduced service was maintained and *Berry Castle* was laid up. In 1917 she was sold for breaking, being finally cut up during the following year. John Jago Tolman became Secretary and Manager of the R.D.S.Co.Ltd. in 1917, and the Company's Registered Office moved from South Embankment to temporary accommodation in his ironmongery shop at The Quay. Three years later the Company moved into their newly purchased Embankment House on South Embankment. The Company's first motor vessel was ordered from Philip's yard in 1921. Named *Berry Castle*, she was a 60ft., twin screw, wooden vessel fitted with twin Thornycroft paraffin/petrol engines. The new boat entered service during 1922.

Compton Castle, pictured at Totnes, was the first R.D.S.Co.Ltd. steamer to be fitted with an elevated passenger deck over her after well deck. Previous steamers used similar structures as boat decks. She was also the first to be built with her upper deck extended out over the paddle sponsons to create far more space for seating.

Compton Castle is pictured below in the 1930s after a wheelhouse and landing platforms were added.

The R.D.S.Co.Ltd.'s first motor vessel, *Berry Castle*, moored at Steamer Quay in the 1920s. Built by Philip's at Dartmouth, she entered service in 1922. Although only 60ft. in length she still boasted two saloons, each furnished with upholstered bench seating. TOTNES MUSEUM SOCIETY.

The village of Dittisham proved a very popular destination for summer visitors but, like Totnes, suffered from adverse landing conditions at low tide. To overcome this the Company embarked upon a major project after the war to construct a pier at Dittisham, which would reach the water even at low tide. Following protracted negotiations with the river authorities and the Admiralty, a 60 year lease was obtained from the Duchy of Cornwall - owners of the river and estuary up to the high water mark. Construction by J. Tribble of Kingswear was completed in 1922. A second motor vessel was built by Philip's during the same year, to operate a shuttle service between the South Embankment and the new pier. She was a small wooden motor boat, appropriately named *Dittisham Castle*.

Sister ships: the *Totnes Castle* and *Kingswear Castle*

At an E.G.M. on 30 July 1923, it was proposed to issue the balance of unissued Ordinary Capital, namely 429 shares at £10 each. The shares were offered to the Company's shareholders in proportion to the Nominal Shares already owned by them. Money was thus raised towards the cost of a new paddle steamer. An order was placed with Philip's for a 108ft. steel paddler, almost identical in design to *Compton Castle*. Philips were also to build her compound, diagonal engines. The new steamer was named *Totnes Castle*. Built from the same drawings and seemingly part of the same contract, a second new paddler was delivered by Philip's during the following year. Named *Kingswear Castle*, she not only replaced the original steamer of the same name, but also inherited her engines. The two new sister ships were built with their main decks extending out over their sponsons, and elevated decks built over their aft well decks. They were additionally supplied with covered wheelhouses and later fitted with landing platforms to help improve boarding

P. S. KINGSWEAR CASTLE of 1924

The hulked *Kingswear Castle* of 1904 forming part of the riverbank at Fleet Mill Quay, downstream of Home Reach, can still be seen today.

accessibility at both South Embankment and Totnes at low water. There was also a slightly raised coach deck running along the centre of the after deck, forming a clerestory to admit more light in the after saloon. They carried 400 passengers and drew just 3ft. of water. Their hulls were 113ft. long (108ft between perpendiculars), 17.8ft. wide, but 28ft. overall when measured across the sponsons.

In 1923 the original *Kingswear Castle*, stripped of her engines and fittings, was sold to the Port Sanitary Authority and converted to serve as an isolation hospital in Dartmouth Harbour until 1927. After attempts to sell her for further use as a houseboat had failed she was eventually hulked at Fleet Mill near Totnes. The unmistakable outline of her hull is still to be seen, embedded into the mud of the riverbank, and pointed out by the skippers of her present day counterparts.

The Company's programme of post war building was completed in 1927 when a third steel vessel was delivered

An early photograph of the *Kingswear Castle* (1924) approaching the river's mouth with Dartmouth Castle and St Petrox Church in the background. She was the last paddle steamer to be built for the company.

River Dart Steamer

Clifton Castle pictured at Hampton Court on the Thames. From 1947 she operated between Westminster and Hampton Court in the ownership of C. H. Whatford & Son. She still works on the river Thames for Collier's Launches of Richmond. G. E. LANGMUIR.

Aboard one of the paddlers, nearing Totnes on 2 September 1936. The awning over the after deck is rolled up to allow the passengers enjoy the sunshine.

from Philip's yard. The new boat, named *Clifton Castle*, was a 70ft. triple screw motor vessel, powered by three Thornycroft paraffin/petrol engines. Her overall deck was interrupted only by two small wooden deckhouses - a combined wheelhouse/saloon companionway and an aft companionway leading to the lavatories and a crew space. The Dart's passenger steamer fleet settled into another of its periodic decades of stability and throughout the 20s and 30s the paddle steamers *Dartmouth Castle*, *Compton Castle*, *Totnes Castle* and *Kingswear Castle* were to establish themselves as an integral part of the picturesque Dart Valley. They were the most distinctive fleet of river paddlers ever to grace an English river, their very shape and characteristic deck arrangement having evolved to suit the nature of the river Dart the only river they were ever designed to ply. The leisurely paddle steamer trip '*Up and Down the Dart*' became a tourist attraction in its

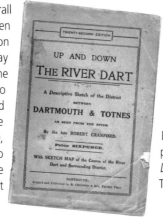

UP AND DOWN THE DART was the motto emblazoned on the paddle boxes of the R.D.S.Co.Ltd. steamers. The phrase was adapted from Robert Cranford's guide book - once available aboard the boats.

own right, and by the 1930s the R.D.S.Co.Ltd. fleet was geared solely to cater for the substantial seasonal tourist trade. Fares to Totnes from Dartmouth during this period were; 1s 9d. single, 3s. return. Cycles were carried at 1s. each way.

Motor cycles were also taken for 3s. each way - but only with empty tanks! Dogs could also enjoy the trip for 6d. Circular excursions were operated in connection with the G.W.R. at Kingswear and Totnes, and with local char-a-banc operators, including Babbacombe Cars, Grey Cars and Comfy Coaches. There were also joint sea and river trips, run in conjunction with the Devon Dock, Pier & Steamship Co. Ltd.'s two sea going paddlers, *Duke of Devonshire* and *Duchess of Devonshire*, which worked out of Exmouth, Teignmouth, Torquay and Plymouth.

On 11 May 1937 an E.C.M. of the R.D.S.Co.Ltd. passed a resolution that the capital of the Company be increased to £30,000 by the creation of 15,000 £1 non voting preference shares. The Chancery Order confirming the alteration to the Memorandum lists William Ball as Chairman, a position he

River Dart P. S. "Totnes Castle"

Totnes Castle (1923) in Dartmouth Harbour prior to the fitting of her landing platforms.

Dartmouth Castle at Dartmouth Regatta in August 1938, pictured as altered, with extended sponson decks and enclosed wheelhouse, to match the newer paddle steamers.

Totnes Castle (outside) and *Kingswear Castle* of 1924 pictured at Totnes in the 1930s.

Kingswear Castle leaving South Embankment in the 1930s.

Kingswear Castle at South Embankment in the 1930s. Ahead is the sea-going paddle steamer DUKE OF DEVONSHIRE.

5534. GREENWAY FERRY, RIVER DART.

Kingswear Castle passing Greenway Quay in the 1930s.

GWR brochure and timetable for combined rail and steamer trips from south Wales in 1938

had held since at least 1923 (he succeeded his father, Wm. Ball Snr, on the Board in 1908). John Percy Tolman was Secretary and Manager, having inherited J. J. Tolman's shares before 1930. George Clift was still a Director and a newcomer to the Board was William Francis Ball.

Some of the capital thus raised was used to finance the construction of a new 44.8ft. wooden, motor vessel in 1937. The *Greenway Castle* was notable in having the shortest Dart career of any R.D.S.Co.Ltd. vessel. In his book *Royal River Highway*, Frank Dix notes that the Ford Motor Company, having established their factory at Dagenham in 1933, encouraged recruitment from Erith on the opposite bank of the river Thames. A contract was signed with A. Gordon Cooper to establish a ferry for the workforce and in 1938 he acquired (perhaps on charter) the new *Greenway Castle* for the purpose. Her history during this period remains vague and various conflicting reports have emerged concerning her career between 1938-1951. However, she certainly reappeared on the Thames after the war and subsequently enjoyed a long life on the river. But not until 1951 do the company records list *Greenway Castle* as '*sold for £509, to Mr. Cooper, Dagenham*'.

KINGSWEAR. 20.882.

Dartmouth Harbour photographed during the mid-30s by Chapman & Son of Dawlish. Laid up in mid stream are three 'Bibby troopers', a familiar sight at Dartmouth between the wars. Nearest to the camera, with the tall funnel is *Lancashire*, *Dorsetshire* is in the middle and *Somersetshire* on the far side. Just departing from Dartmouth, on the left of the picture, is one of Dartmouth Council's Kingswear passenger ferries. The other two are moored off Waterhead Creek, on the Kingswear side. At Kingswear one of the Lower Ferry pontoons manoeuvres into the slip, while a second waits off the Railway Ferry pontoon landing. Nearest the Dartmouth shore *Kingswear Castle* heads up stream after visiting the two castles at the harbour mouth, while an empty *Totnes Castle* steams astern to clear the troopships and possibly moor off Waterhead Creek near *Dartmouth Castle*, which can be seen behind *Lancashire*'s foremast. The underwater electricity cable between Bayards Cove and Kingswear can be detected.

Second World War

The building of a second motor vessel only months later in 1938 seems to lend support to Mr Dix's account regarding *Greenway Castle*. Like her, the 60ft. *Seymour Castle* was also built by Messrs Ferris and Bank at the Creekside Boatyard in Old Mill Creek, Dartmouth, at a cost of £2,079 but her immediate career was suddenly curtailed on the 3 September 1939, when all pleasure cruises on the Dart ceased following the declaration of war against Germany. *Totnes Castle* was initially hired for use as a liberty boat at Devonport Dockyard, but during 1940 both *Totnes Castle* and *Kingswear Castle* were moored on the Kingswear side of the river. *Dittisham Castle* was sold in 1940 to Dartmouth Coaling Company. The remainder of the fleet was laid up in Old Mill Creek. During 1941 permission was obtained to maintain a limited summer service to Totnes with the *Totnes Castle*. In his book *A Shipman's Tale*, T. W. E. Roche recalls:

> The first day was a fiasco, because something went wrong with the boilers and she never left her moorings, but they soon put that right and she was to be seen at the pontoon or alongside the Embankment taking on board the visitors - an astonishing contrast with the grey painted merchant ships entering the harbour in convoy. Yet there was something uplifting to those of us who earned their bread and butter among those ships when, on a warm summer evening of 1941, as we clambered down the umpteenth rope ladder, to hear the plash of paddles and, looking over our shoulders to behold the well filled decks of TOTNES CASTLE, the only ship in peace-time colouring we were destined to see for years.

Roche also notes that the trips continued into October and that *Kingswear Castle* sometimes deputised for *Totnes Castle*. Both steamers occasionally relieved *The Mew* on the railway ferry. The opportunity to stand in for the ferry steamer came early during the war, when in May 1940, *The Mew* answered the call to help at Dunkirk. Her volunteer G.W.R. crew steamed 'full ahead' to Dover for over 24 hours, only to learn that the ferry was considered unsuitable for the beach work at Dunkirk, and was given permission to return to Dartmouth.

The *Seymour Castle* meanwhile was based at Ramsgate and employed by the Admiralty in marking swept channels. She experienced more success in reaching Dunkirk, although she never actually ventured into the beaches.

In 1942 *Clifton Castle* was sold to the Crown and seems to have been used on the river Avon. After the war in 1947 she was moored at Bowling Harbour on the Clyde and later purchased by C. H. Whatford & Sons on the Thames for their Westminster-Hampton Court run. During 1944, when the Allied invasion force was gathering along the South Coast, *Kingswear Castle* found employment as a tender for the US Navy in Dartmouth Harbour. She had also been used as a naval stores at Dittisham Pier. *Compton Castle* was used by the naval authorities as an ammunition carrier. *Dartmouth Castle* remained laid up for the duration and was in such poor condition after the war that the Company decided to replace her. However, she never left Old Mill Creek, her hull can still be seen there, forming a retaining wall at Creekside Boatyard, in buried company, so it is rumoured, of even older hulked steamers. *Berry Castle* was sold in 1947, leaving the Dart for future use by a petroleum company in Holland.

Dartmouth Castle buried in the river bank in Old Mill Creek.

One of a series of photographs taken by L. H. Hobbs in 1947 for publicity purposes.
Totnes Castle (left) and *Kingswear Castle* steam downstream into Dartmouth Harbour.

The Welsh connection

The River Dart Steamboat Co.Ltd.'s excursions resumed after the war with the three paddlers: *Compton Castle, Totnes Castle* and *Kingswear Castle*, and the motor vessel *Seymour Castle*. In 1948 *Dartmouth Castle*'s replacement was launched from Philip's yard. She was an 85ft. steel, screw, motor vessel, powered by twin Gleniffer diesel engines. She cost £11,331 and was fitted with her predecessors wheelhouse and lifeboat. She also took the paddler's name. A second new motor vessel was completed by Philip's during the following year at a cost of £10,522. This was the 67ft. steel, screw, *Berry Castle*, which effectively replaced her earlier namesake.

The Annual Return of the R.D.S.Co.Ltd. for 1949 lists the Directors as: John Percy Tolman, Managing Director; William Francis Ball, Secretary; Henry Frederick Ball; George Clift; and Richard Leslie Dennis. Tolman's death on 19 November 1950, ended his family's long association with the management of the Company's steamers, a link that stretched back to the foundation of the Dartmouth & Torbay Steam Packet Company in 1877. The position of Managing Director was filled by R. L. Dennis, who was also Chairman of Dartmouth Harbour Commission, a director in various coal shipping companies and Manager of the Torbay & Brixham Coaling Co. Ltd. It was through his Welsh business connections in his coal interests, that a takeover of the R.D.S.Co.Ltd. was successfully completed during the summer of 1952.

At separate General Meetings of Preference and Ordinary Shareholders on 31 July 1952, Extraordinary Resolutions were passed.

That sanction be given to the payment by Evans & Reid Investment Co. Ltd. of compensation for loss of office to the undermentioned Directors of the amounts set opposite their names on the resignation of their office as Directors of the Company, provided that sale and purchase of shares in the Company shall proceed to completion in accordance with the terms of a circular letter dated 4th July 1952, issued by the Company and submitting an offer to purchase the shares of and in the Company by Evans & Reid Investment Co.Ltd.

The compensation was: Major W. F. Ball - £1,900; Mr. G. Clift - £700; Mr. H. F. Ball - £550. On 6 August 1952 Major W. F. Ball resigned his Secretaryship to P. P. Manley of Paignton and, together with George Clift and H. F. Ball, who resigned their positions in the R.D.S.Co.Ltd. on the same day, ended his family's links with the Company that began in 1877 when William Ball and the original syndicate of shareholders first acquired the Dartmouth Steam Packet Co.Ltd.'s fleet of river steamers.

Seymour Castle of 1938 (nearest) pictured in the 1960s with the *Berry Castle* of 1949 at Totnes.

Boarding the *Totnes Castle* on Dartmouth's South Embankment, in the 1950s. P.S.P.S. ARCHIVES

The new Board of Directors as at 29 August 1952 were: Chairman - Trevor Llewellyn Price of Porthcawl, an Incorporated Accountant; Charles Jackson Evans of Newport, Mon., Shipowner; Alexander Charles Grant of Llanishen, Glamorgan, Shipowner; and Newton Lloyd Wade of Newport, Solicitor. All were Directors of Evans & Reid Investment Co. Ltd., of Empire House, Mount Stuart Square, Cardiff, which had acquired 1,199 Ordinary Shares and 9,845 Preference Shares in the R.D.S.Co.Ltd. R. L. Dennis was still Managing Director. The Directors' Report for 1952 formally notified shareholders that Evans & Reid Investment Co.Ltd. had acquired controlling interest in the River Dart Steamboat Co. Ltd. However, old associations lingered a while longer through the small shareholdings retained by the Bartlett family and George Clift, while Katherine Mary Tolman still held 2,270 Preference Shares. Over the next 25 years the new executive initially employed a programme of fleet modernisation,

Compton Castle heading down the Dart in the 1950s.

The Mew on the Railway Ferry in the early 1950s.

coupled with the steady sale of fixed assets. But later, declining profits led to the gradual sale of the boats and the eventual withdrawal of passenger services altogether.

The end of an era on the Railway Ferry

At midnight on 31 December 1947 the 'Big Four' railway companies were nationalised and *The Mew* passed to the ownership of British Rail

Kingswear Castle in Dartmouth Harbour in the 1960s.
P.S.P.S. ARCHIVES

FOR YOUR OUTING
VISIT DEVON'S BEAUTIFUL

RIVER DART

12 MILES OF WONDERFUL SCENERY

FROM TOTNES TO DARTMOUTH
OR VICE VERSA
ON A PADDLE STEAMER
OR MOTOR CRUISER
OPERATED BY

The River Dart Steamboat Co. Ltd.
EMBANKMENT HOUSE, DARTMOUTH

Western Region. Under a long standing agreement originally made with the G.W.R., a R.D.S.Co.Ltd. paddler, usually *Totnes Castle*, deputised for the ferry steamer during her annual maintenance. In December 1953 Leslie Herbert Hobbs succeeded P. P. Manley as the R.D.S.Co.Ltd. Secretary, and one of his first tasks was to re-negotiate this charter agreement with British Rail (BR). The new contract stipulated that the R.D.S.Co.Ltd. had to provide a boat, even in the summer months if required. BR also agreed that the vessel would be one of the river Dart company's paddlers. Paddington seemingly did not appreciate the size or cost of operation of the steamers in question - especially in respect of infrequent winter trains carrying no more than a handful of passengers.

Since 1952 Board of Trade (B.O.T.) surveys on *The Mew* had indicated an imminent programme of replating and in 1954 it was decided to withdraw the steamer at the end of the summer season, rather than proceeding with expensive repairs. She made her last trip amid an emotional farewell of rockets and ships' sirens on 8 October and following a few months laid up in Plymouth's Millbay Docks, was sold for scrap in 1955.

Kingswear Castle at South Embankment in the 1960s.
P.S.P.S. ARCHIVES

Kingswear Castle at South Embankment in the 1960s. P.S.P.S. ARCHIVES

The R.D.S.Co.Ltd.'s records for 1954 note a sudden decline in revenue for relief ferry work following the withdrawal of *The Mew*. Realising the expense incurred in chartering one of the R.D.S.Co.Ltd.'s paddlers, BR exercised a clause in their agreement which permitted them to hire from another company. They sought a more economic charter and selected the Millbrook Steamboat & Trading Co.Ltd.'s 50 ft, motor vessel *Lady Elizabeth* for the purpose. It was at last appreciated by BR that such an economic vessel was a viable proposition for the Railway Ferry. The R.D.S.Co.Ltd, re-negotiated their contract with BR and their *Seymour Castle* was eventually supplied on a time-charter. In 1956 BR ordered two 57.9ft. wood, screw, motor vessels from Blackmore & Sons of Bideford to take over the ferry service. The new boats were named *Adrian Gilbert* and *Humphrey Gilbert* at a special naming ceremony at Kingswear on 18 March 1957. They were immediately employed on the Kingswear Ferry, The R.D.S.Co.Ltd's charter and long association with the Railway Ferry officially ended on 26 July 1957.

The three post-war paddle steamers together at Totnes shortly before *Compton Castle*'s withdrawal at the end of 1962. *Compton Castle* is moored at Steamer Quay with *Kingswear Castle* alongside. *Totnes Castle* has turned downstream.

46/14

The paddle steamers are withdrawn

The new Board of Directors of the R.D.S.Co.Ltd. took stock of the Company's assets. Their 1952 Report lists the fixed assets as: Embankment House, Dittisham Pier and ticket office, Old Mill and Old Mill Slipway, and Totnes Quay, which included a kiosk and the row of warehouses. Over the next five years the Company sold Nos. 1 & 2 warehouses and 'parking land' at Bridgetown Quay. The remaining warehouses were sold to Totnes Corporation in 1959. The waiting room at Dittisham was sold and £3,500 was put in reserve for repairs to Dittisham Pier, which had suffered from wartime neglect. The repairs were never undertaken and after several years of disuse by the Company, and with the lease from the Duchy due to expire in 1982, the Company opted to sell the pier. It was sold in 1964 to Richard Dimbleby and Mrs. B. Ross-Esson of Dittisham for their personal use and survives today, shortened from its original length. The boats listed in the 1952 report were the motor vessels *Seymour Castle, Dartmouth Castle* and *Berry Castle*. Less depreciation they were valued collectively £17,311. But the paddle steamers *Totnes Castle, Kingswear Castle* and *Compton Castle*, were only valued at a collective break-up value of £797!

R. L. Dennis and C. J. Evans died during 1958, and A. C. Grant resigned from the Board in March of the same year. The Company Secretary, L. H. Hobbs was appointed as a Director. A second new Director, Archibald Gomer Davies of Barry, was appointed in 1961. He was Secretary of Evans & Reid Investment Co. Ltd. and also a Director of the Devon Star Shipping Co. Ltd. On 31 March 1961 T. L. Price, N. L. Wade, and L. H. Hobbs were also appointed as Directors of the Devon Star Shipping Co.Ltd., following the purchase of a controlling interest in that Company by the R.D.S.Co.Ltd. The new acquisition included a booking office and embarkation facilities at Princess Pier, Torquay, together with the 81ft. passenger motor vessel *Torbay Prince*. The takeover was '*for the purpose of engaging in the pleasure cruising trade from Torquay*'. The new venture, however, was short lived and the D.S.S.Co.Ltd. shares were sold in 1964 but an amicable

Torbay Prince in Torbay during the 1950s.

business contact was maintained and through bookings were introduced for the *Torbay Prince* and R.D.S.Co.Ltd. vessels.

At the end of the 1962 season the Ministry of Transport (M.O.T.) surveyor reported that he was unable to renew *Compton Castle*'s passenger certificate for 1963 unless extensive repairs were undertaken. The R.D.S.Co.Ltd., deciding against repair, placed an order with Philip's for a replacement. The new boat was to be a steel, twin screw, motor vessel with a 400 passenger capacity - for delivery in May 1963. The cost was estimated at £30,000 and £2,000 was immediately paid on account. The new 100ft. vessel was launched on 25 March 1963 and named *Conway Castle* by Mrs. T. L. Price. The boat was fitted out with *Compton Castle*'s wheelhouse and deckrails, while that steamer remained laid up, offered for sale. In June 1964 *Compton Castle* was sold to Messrs Bourne and Woods for future use as a museum and cafe at Kingsbridge where, in 1971, she featured in a Birds Eye advert and an episode of the Onedin Line. Outlasting successive owners and schemes in Kingsbridge, Looe and Truro, and seemingly reluctant to totally disappear, the hull of *Compton Castle* survives today, serving as a platform for successive retail ventures at Truro's Lemon Quay.

While *Compton Castle* had remained laid up in the Dart during 1963, an inspection of *Totnes Castle* revealed repairs

Captain Rundles (left) on the bridge of the motor vessel *Conway Castle* beside the paddle steamer *Compton Castle*'s wheelhouse.

Compton Castle was moored at Kingsbridge between 1964 and 1978, employed as a café.

requiring a minimum £6,000 expenditure. Once again the Directors decided against repair. Advantage was taken of a Government Loan Scheme for the building of a new vessel. A £25,000 loan was agreed, to be repaid over ten years. Bolson of Poole were nominated to build the boat - a sister ship to *Conway Castle* - at an estimated cost of £33,000, for delivery in June 1964. She was launched from Bolson's in May 1964 by Mrs. N. L. Wade, and named *Cardiff Castle*. Delivery was taken on 4 July and she was in service during the following week.

Cardiff Castle being launched at Poole in 1964. BERNARD COX

Totnes Castle's wheelhouse and lifeboat were transferred to the new motor vessel. In April 1964, following her sale to a sailing school in the river Dart, the *Totnes Castle* was converted to an accommodation vessel for 38 people, with a large white superstructure obliterating virtually everything above the hull. Owing to the ill health of her new owner, however, the venture failed and within a year she was up for sale again. She remained at her moorings, slowly deteriorating, until in November 1967 she was sold for breaking at Demelweek &

Totnes Castle as an accommodation vessel in 1965. BERNARD COX

Kingswear Castle at South Embankment, Dartmouth, in 1963, the sole operating paddle steamer of the River Dart Steamboat Co. Ltd. The second building from the left is Embankment House, the headquarters of the River Dart Steamboat Co. Ltd. from 1920 until 1976. P.S.P.S. ARCHIVES

Kingswear Castle approaching Totnes on 7 July 1965, just a few weeks before she was withdrawn from service. BERNARD COX

Kingswear Castle laid up in Old Mill Creek in 1966, alongside the hulk of the paddle steamer *Dartmouth Castle* of 1907. BERNARD COX

Redding's scrapyard on Marrowbone Slip in Plymouth's Sutton Harbour. Maintaining the characteristic reluctance of the R.D.S.Co.Ltd.'s paddlers to be scrapped, *Totnes Castle* never reached the breakers. The *Western Morning News* for 11 November 1967 reports:

> *The veteran paddle steamer* TOTNES CASTLE *being towed from Dartmouth to Plymouth on her last voyage to the breakers, sank in bad weather in Bigbury Bay on Thursday (9th November 1967). The* TOTNES CASTLE *was being towed by the Plymouth tug* ANTONY. *No one was aboard her when she foundered in heavy seas in about 20 fathoms. The seven man crew of the* ANTONY *had time to cast off and retrieve their towing hawser before the paddle steamer went down. A spokesman for* ANTONY*'s owners, W. J. Reynolds of Torpoint, told last night that the two steamers set off in good weather on the five hour voyage, but ran into heavy seas which sprang up quickly off Burgh Island.*

Years later *Totnes Castle*'s bell turned up in a Bristol antique shop and was purchased by Totnes Museum where it remains on display.

The Company's sole remaining paddle steamer, *Kingswear Castle*, had undergone major repairs, including the renewal of the boiler in 1962 and replacement of some hull plates. Due to her 1961 repairs her book value was £1,575 - she had cost £10,333 to build. In 1964 she completed her season on 22 September, but in the following year she finished at the end of August. Fares during 1965 were increased by 10%, but wet and stormy conditions throughout the summer had reduced passenger loadings.The Directors' Report for the year ending 1965 sadly announced:

> *It is with some regret the Directors report that the one remaining paddle steamer* KINGSWEAR CASTLE *ended her period of running in August. The vessel is 42 years of age and has become quite uneconomic to maintain or operate and will be disposed of at the first advantageous opportunity. The Company's fleet, now entirely diesel engined, provide better operating facilities which have enabled additional services to be scheduled for 1966 without the replacement of the paddle steamer.*

Demise of the River Dart Steamboat Co.Ltd

An ominous litany of excuses set the tone for poor figures in Annual Reports in the latter half of the 1960s. 1967 was a particularly bad year, weather conditions between April and June, and for September/October, included gales at Dartmouth and flooding at Totnes. Twenty four days sailngs had to be cancelled. Revenue remained sufficient to meet dividends on Preference Shares, but until the mid 1970s Directors were to forego their fees.

The Board of Directors during this period were: L. H. Hobbs, Managing Director and Secretary, A. G. Davies and Lt. Col. N. L. Wade OBE. T.D., who succeeded the Chairmanship following T. L. Price's death in 1967. As Directors of Evans & Reid Investment Co. Ltd., Davies and Wade held additional directorships in some 25 of that Company's other business interests. Many of these were South Wales coal and shipping companies, and in 1972 a pilot boat was acquired and registered in the ownership of the R.D.S.Co.Ltd., 'to engage in inter-group pilot boat chartering to fellow subsidiary companies'. The boat was named *Leslie H*, after Leslie Herbert Hobbs who resigned from the Board in 1971.

Meanwhile revenue from the five passenger boats continued to deteriorate. Operating receipts for 1972 were £3,000 down on the previous year. A loss of £1,000 on the passenger side was only balanced by receipts from the pilot boat *Leslie H*. In the Autumn of 1972 *Berry Castle* and *Seymour Castle* were put up for sale.

Berry Castle was initially sold to Fareham owners, but was later acquired by Dart Pleasure Craft Ltd. and returned to the Dart, renamed *Totnes Castle*. She survived on the river until 1985 when she was sold to Plymouth Boat Cruises Ltd. for use in the Plymouth district. She currently plies Ullswater in the Lake District, beautifully rebuilt and renamed *Lady Wakefield*.

Seymour Castle was sold to Tony and Hilary Soper who renamed her *Scomber* and used her to operate bird watching and natural history cruises on the Tamar and Dart rivers. After a further spell at Plymouth in the ownership of K. T. Bridge, during which time she suffered the name *Southern Comfort of Plymstock*, she also returned to the Dart. Her new owner, G. H. Ridall, thankfully renamed her *Dartmothian* in recognition of her origins - she was built in Old Mill Creek, Dartmouth and constructed from grown timbers taken from the surrounding woods. She currently plies the river Thames from Reading as the *Devon Belle*.

Directors continued to forego their fees and from 1972

Ex-*Berry Castle* moored at Glenridding on Ullswater in the Lake District in 2012 as the *Lady Wakefield*.

Thames Rivercruise's *Devon Belle*, Ex-*Seymour Castle*, on the Thames at Reading in 2012.

Preference Share payments were deferred. There had been no payment on Ordinary Shares for many years. New appointments to the Board in 1973 were, Thomas Eifon Williams of Dartmouth, Gerald Devins of Cardiff and David Kenneth Hugh Martin of Cowbridge, Glamorgan. Profits for 1973 increased by £1,900, but £1,600 of this was attributed directly to the pilot boat operation. In 1974 an additional pilot boat was acquired, named *Archie D*, after Archibald Gomer Davies, who retired from the R.D.S.Co.Ltd. board during the same year. The turnover for pleasure boat operations in 1974 was £25,202, while the inter-group pilot boat charters totalled £10,000. The book values of the Company's vessels were listed as: *Dartmouth Castle* £685, *Conway Castle* £21,913, *Cardiff Castle* £25,949, *Leslie H* £12,719, *Archie D* £28,010. A note below this entry on the Balance Sheet indicated the fate awaiting the passenger fleet - '*The potential sales proceeds of the three Castle vessels are, on the cessation of pleasure boat operations, considered to be in excess of total book written down value as at 31 December 1974.*'

The Directors Report for 1974 announced:

> *The principal activities of the Company have been the operation of pleasure boats on the River Dart and hiring out and charter of pilot vessels. But due to economic circumstances the Directors regretfully decided that it is necessary to discontinue as operators of pleasure boats, which will not run in 1975 or subsequently.*

The Millbrook Steamboat & Trading Co. Ltd. purchased *Dartmouth Castle* in 1975, but the other two boats remained laid up. Ownership of the two pilot boats was also officially transferred to the fellow subsidiary company that had been operating them. In the following year the River Dart Steamboat Co. Ltd. moved their Registered Office to the Shipyard, Old Mill Creek, and at a meeting of shareholders in Brixham in the same year it was agreed to change the Company's name to the River Dart Boat & Leisure Co.Ltd.

During the winter of 1976/7 *Dartmouth Castle* was re-sold by the Millbrook company to Dart Pleasure Craft Ltd., which effectively became the R.D.S.Co.Ltd.'s successor. *Conway Castle* was sold to Gloucester Shipping Co. Ltd. and continues to provide cruises along the river Severn between Worcester and Tewkesbury. Finally on 20 January 1977, exactly 100 years since the original Dartmouth & Torbay Steam Packet Company had acquired Charles Seale Hayne's fleet of paddlers, the R.D.S.Co.Ltd.'s last passenger boat *Cardiff Castle*, was sold to the Millbrook Steamboat & Trading Co. Ltd.

Dartmouth Castle during her second spell at Plymouth in 1984.

Severn Leisure Cruises' *Conway Castle* on the river Severn in August 2011.

Kingswear Castle's restoration underway on the Medway. P.S.P.S. ARCHIVES

4

THE *KINGSWEAR CASTLE* IS SAVED

After a very short final season, the River Dart Steamship Co. Ltd's last paddle steamer, *Kingswear Castle*, was withdrawn from passenger service at the end of August 1965 and laid up in Old Mill Creek alongside the hulk of the former *Dartmouth Castle*. The Paddle Steamer Preservation Society, which had been formed in 1959, immediately showed an interest in the ship, realising that her relatively small size and the fact that she had been reboilered and extensively replated in 1961, made her the most suitable remaining British candidate for preservation and eventual restoration to commercial operation. The Society, however, was then only six years old and had a small membership and insufficient resources to both purchase and restore the ship. At their Annual General Meeting in November 1965, therefore, it was decided to defer any attempt to purchase her whilst attempts were made to find someone who might charter her from the Society and put her to good use until further funds could be generated. A fund-raising appeal was launched and by the time of the November 1966 A.G.M. a decision had been made to go ahead with the purchase. The River Dart Steamboat Co.Ltd. generously agreed to sell *Kingswear Castle* for a mere £600 due to '*sentiment and the fact that the old vessel is the last of the line*' and a charterer was found in the form of Alan & Colin Ridett's Medway Queen Marina, on the river Medina in the Isle of Wight.

On 20 June 1967 the steamer was formally purchased by Paddle Steam Navigation Ltd., an operating company set up by the P.S.P.S. for that purpose, and she was immediately slipped at the R.D.S.Co.Ltd.'s Old Mill Creek yard for bottom painting

Kingswear Castle arriving at the Medway Marina on the river Medina.
P.S.P.S. ARCHIVES

and closing-up prior to her departure for the Isle of Wight. The charter to Ridett's came into force on 3 August 1967, thus relieving the Society of the responsibility and expense of arranging the tow. *Kingswear Castle* finally left the Dart in tow of a motor launch which took her as far as Brixham where the tow was transferred to the trawler *Auchmore* for the voyage up-channel to Cowes, where she arrived on 28 August 1967. She was then moved up the river Medina to a mooring off Ridett's marina near Binfield, where she joined the former coastal paddle steamer *Medway Queen*, which was already in use as a club ship and restaurant.

Small working parties of Society members did their best to keep the ship in good order but their efforts were frustrated partly by lack of professional equipment and expertise and partly by the inaccessibility of the ship in her muddy, mid-river berth. The Ridett's engineer kept the engines in good order and during 1969 the *Kingswear Castle* skippered by Harry Spencer of Cowes, made two forays into the Solent under her

Kingswear Castle, with a damaged paddle box, pictured from Cowes floating bridge on the river Medina in 1969. JERRY LEWIS, P.S.P.S. ARCHIVES

own steam. On the weekend of 3-4 May she ran trials off Cowes, and on 8 June crossed to the mainland and steamed up the Beaulieu river to Bucklers Hard. On the latter outing she was filmed from the air for the BBC TV's *Bird's Eye View* series. In the spring of 1970 she was moved from her river mooring onto a mud berth on the river bank between Binfield and Folly Inn, where she quickly fell prey to vandalism. Her attractive etched glass saloon windows were smashed, her builders plate removed and thrown overboard (to be recovered later by a passer-by and returned) and various other damage caused. The Ridett's, who were experiencing other difficulties with their marina development, had still failed to announce any firm plans for her use and with the ship's condition quickly and visibly deteriorating it was clear that some hard thinking was called for.

In the autumn, the P.S.P.S. central committee announced that the charter agreement with the Ridetts had been terminated and that henceforth the Society would take direct responsibility for the ship, which was to be moved to a new berth at the Medway Bridge Marina at Rochester on the river Medway. *Kingswear Castle* was towed downstream to Cowes on 6 October 1970 to spend the winter at Amey Marine's Shamblers Yard where she was again closed up and her forward well decked over in preparation for the long coastal tow. She finally departed from Cowes on 16 June 1971 in the charge of the tug *Dagger* and, having called at Newhaven for the night arrived safely on the Medway on 18 June, just a few hours ahead of the force 6-8 gales which struck the south east coast that evening.

The cost of the tow was a severe drain on the Society's resources and very little cash was left with which to begin the restoration work so, in December 1972, the Society's officers felt duty-bound to recommend her sale to the highest bidder. Happily, their suggestion was rejected and acted as a much needed spur to activity. At the same meeting a representative of the Sydney Maritime Museum was present with an offer to purchase the paddle steamer and take her to Australia - which further galvanised people into action. Lawrie Beale was appointed as Restoration Project Leader and a small hard-working band of volunteers pushed the work slowly ahead. Over the next seven or eight years much was achieved: The paddle wheels were removed for replacement; the shafts drawn; decking replaced or re-caulked; some hull plates and frames were reinforced; wasted steel work replaced; and much more. Throughout it all the engines and boilers received steady attention and, at the end of January 1977 steam was raised for the first time since the ship left the Medina.

Kingswear Castle undergoing restoration and renewal on the river Medway. BERNIE THOMPSON, RODDY MCKEE AND P.S.P.S. ARCHIVES

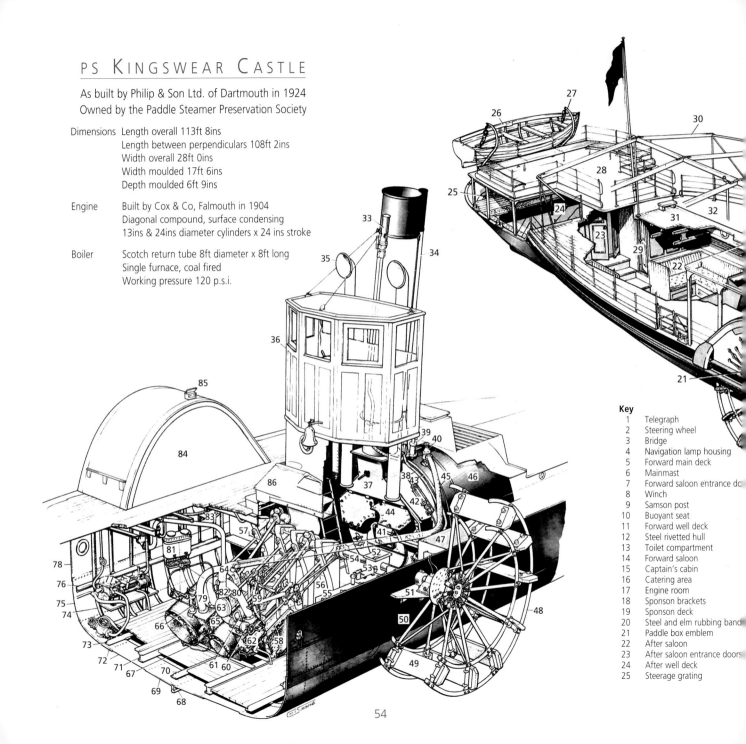

ps KINGSWEAR CASTLE

As built by Philip & Son Ltd. of Dartmouth in 1924
Owned by the Paddle Steamer Preservation Society

Dimensions Length overall 113ft 8ins
Length between perpendiculars 108ft 2ins
Width overall 28ft 0ins
Width moulded 17ft 6ins
Depth moulded 6ft 9ins

Engine Built by Cox & Co, Falmouth in 1904
Diagonal compound, surface condensing
13ins & 24ins diameter cylinders x 24 ins stroke

Boiler Scotch return tube 8ft diameter x 8ft long
Single furnace, coal fired
Working pressure 120 p.s.i.

Key
1   Telegraph
2   Steering wheel
3   Bridge
4   Navigation lamp housing
5   Forward main deck
6   Mainmast
7   Forward saloon entrance do
8   Winch
9   Samson post
10 Buoyant seat
11 Forward well deck
12 Steel rivetted hull
13 Toilet compartment
14 Forward saloon
15 Captain's cabin
16 Catering area
17 Engine room
18 Sponson brackets
19 Sponson deck
20 Steel and elm rubbing band
21 Paddle box emblem
22 After saloon
23 After saloon entrance doors
24 After well deck
25 Steerage grating

54

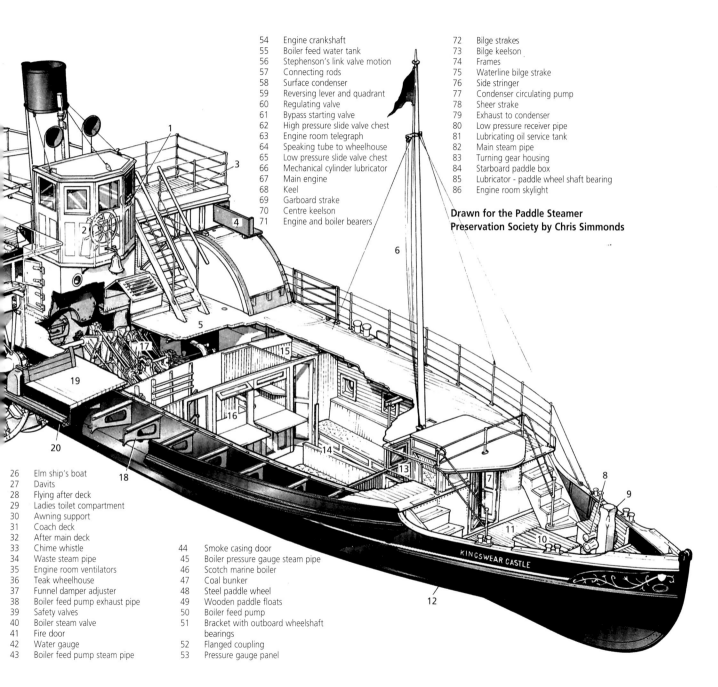

54 Engine crankshaft
55 Boiler feed water tank
56 Stephenson's link valve motion
57 Connecting rods
58 Surface condenser
59 Reversing lever and quadrant
60 Regulating valve
61 Bypass starting valve
62 High pressure slide valve chest
63 Engine room telegraph
64 Speaking tube to wheelhouse
65 Low pressure slide valve chest
66 Mechanical cylinder lubricator
67 Main engine
68 Keel
69 Garboard strake
70 Centre keelson
71 Engine and boiler bearers

72 Bilge strakes
73 Bilge keelson
74 Frames
75 Waterline bilge strake
76 Side stringer
77 Condenser circulating pump
78 Sheer strake
79 Exhaust to condenser
80 Low pressure receiver pipe
81 Lubricating oil service tank
82 Main steam pipe
83 Turning gear housing
84 Starboard paddle box
85 Lubricator - paddle wheel shaft bearing
86 Engine room skylight

Drawn for the Paddle Steamer Preservation Society by Chris Simmonds

26 Elm ship's boat
27 Davits
28 Flying after deck
29 Ladies toilet compartment
30 Awning support
31 Coach deck
32 After main deck
33 Chime whistle
34 Waste steam pipe
35 Engine room ventilators
36 Teak wheelhouse
37 Funnel damper adjuster
38 Boiler feed pump exhaust pipe
39 Safety valves
40 Boiler steam valve
41 Fire door
42 Water gauge
43 Boiler feed pump steam pipe

44 Smoke casing door
45 Boiler pressure gauge steam pipe
46 Scotch marine boiler
47 Coal bunker
48 Steel paddle wheel
49 Wooden paddle floats
50 Boiler feed pump
51 Bracket with outboard wheelshaft bearings
52 Flanged coupling
53 Pressure gauge panel

In 1979 the Society decided to divert more funds to the ship in order to allow steel plating and other work to be carried out by professional contractors This acted to redouble enthusiasm and the volunteer workforce increased and discovered a new dynamism. Valuable assistance was received from firms who gave materials free of charge or at cost and the restoration forged ahead. On 20 November 1982, the boiler was steamed and the engines turned for the first time in thirteen years. By 21 July 1983 the ship passed her hull survey and then, on on the weekend of 4-6 November came the crowning glory - *Kingswear Castle* successfully completed her steaming and manoeuvring trials in the river Medway. The job was virtually complete.

Steaming trials of *Kingswear Castle*, November 1983. P.S.P.S. ARCHIVES

5

The Medway years

After a winter spent on further work *Kingswear Castle* was able to re-enter commercial service albeit on a very limited scale and carrying a maximum of twelve passengers. A number of Thames and Medway pilots, together with John Megoran volunteered to act as skippers on a rota basis. The engine room was manned by Chris Jones, while other volunteers looked after the deck and catering departments. During the Easter holiday period and from 16 June until 16 September 1984 she sailed on an average of one or two days each week on public and charter cruises along the Medway from Strood Pier. On non-operational days the ship lay alongside at Medway Bridge Marina where two volunteers generated both income and interest by providing afternoon teas, dinner parties and guided tours whilst doubling as unpaid ship keepers. On 22 April she made a sailing to greet the Dunkirk veteran paddle steamer *Medway Queen*, which was making an emotional return to Chatham atop a large submersible pontoon after a long exile in the Isle of Wight. On 23 June, in what was to prove the first of many visits, *Kingswear Castle* ventured round to the Thames, touching at Southend Pier en route, to become the 'star attraction' at the Gravesend Edwardian Fair. The high spots of the season came on 9 and 16 September when she steamed out into the Medway to rendezvous with the P.S.P.S.'s other vessel, the sea going paddle steamer *Waverley*. These were the first occasions for fifteen years that two operational paddle steamers had met in British waters and were to be repeated almost annually for the next 28 seasons.

Kingswear Castle's first season was technically a great success and represented a triumph for her volunteer crew and for the restoration team but it was clear to the directors of Paddle Steam Navigation Ltd, the company set up to own and operate the ship on behalf of the P.S.P.S., that for continued

John Megoran appointed as full time skipper of *Kingswear Castle* a position he would fill for the next twenty eight years. P.S.P.S. ARCHIVES

operation to become financially viable, the only long-term solution was to obtain a full passenger certificate in order to carry paying loads. Close consideration was given to returning the ship to the river Dart to operate in conjunction with one of the established companies there, but in the end it was decided to keep the ship on the Medway, within easy reach of the vast population of London and the south east of England, and offer an expanded programme of public sailings based on her experimental 1984 season. John Megoran was appointed full time master and manager. An agreement was reached with the embryonic Chatham Historic Dockyard Trust for the ship to operate from Thunderbolt Pier within the former Royal Dockyard where storage and office facilities would also be made available.

Kingswear Castle was slipped at Crescent Shipyard, Rochester, in November 1984 for a full D.T.I. (Department of

Trade & Industry) survey. While she was out of the water the hull was sandblasted and painted, free of charge, by one of the many supportive local firms. Some hull plates were replaced and the ship returned to her lay-up berth where, throughout the winter, work continued on the engine, the fitting of additional life-saving apparatus, a new generator, porthole deadlights, emergency escape hatches and on up-grading the saloons.

By 16 May 1985 the ship had been issued with a Class 5 certificate which permitted her to carry 250 passengers on the Medway and the Thames above Gravesend, and a Class 6 for 100 in the more exposed Thames estuary, but was not allowed to carry passengers across Sea Reach between the Medway and Southend. Two days later *Kingswear Castle* backed away from Thunderbolt Pier on a charter to the Coastal Cruising Association, her first cruise with a full D.T.I. passenger certificate for twenty years, followed the next day by her first public excursion. Her core programme consisted of public Medway cruises from Thunderbolt and Strood piers and four sailings each Thursday from Southend. The latter were extremely well patronised but, despite extensive advertising, the Medway trips were poorly supported. By mid-season the Medway trips had been reduced to two days per week, but

Sunday 19 May 1985, *Kingswear Castle*'s first full scale public excursion for 19 years. P.S.P.S. ARCHIVES

Kingswear Castle and Tower Bridge. STAFFORD ELLERMAN

income was boosted by private charters and a number of exciting special cruises. At the end of June she went to Gravesend once again to view the barge match and take part in the Edwardian Fair before sailing on through Tower Bridge and into the heart of London on 1 July. After a couple of days running trips from Tower Pier she entered the West India Docks to take centre stage in the Docklands Fundays event. Back on the Medway: she ran special sailings between 20 and 24 July to view the competitors in the Tall Ships Race; made her first trip up river towards Snodland on 4 August; and sailed through the Swale to rendezvous with *Waverley* in Whitstable harbour on 21 September. Her season ended on 13 October, and it was a testament to her crew that, despite poor weather, difficulties sourcing suitable steam coal and some problems with fire bars in the boiler, the ship had lost only one sailing due mechanical problems.

During the winter of 1985-86 another invitation was received to take the ship back to the river Dart to run in conjunction with the Dart Valley Railway. The prospect of running on six days per week within an established operation on her home river held great appeal, and consideration was even given to running *Kingswear Castle* on the Medway during April, May and June before undertaking a coast-hugging journey to the Dart for the high season, returning home again in September. In the end practicalities ruled the plan out, but

Rendezvous with the sea going paddle steamer WAVERLEY on 28 September 1986. *Kingswear Castle* with her new landing platforms. JOHN GOSS

it was one which was to raise its head from time to time over the next twenty five years.

In a further move to protect the ship's long term financial future a new company, Kingswear Castle Excursions Ltd. was formed to operate the vessel on charter from Paddle Steam Navigation (P.S.N). The aim was to ensure that, should adverse trading conditions lead to the bankruptcy of the trading company, the ship would revert to its owners, P.S.N., and hopefully avoid the clutches of any creditors.

During the winter more work was carried out on the engine, inner funnel, decks and saloons. A new set of modified fire bars were fitted to the boiler and *Kingswear Castle* emerged to start her 1986 season with a new mast, green boot-topping (i.e. corrosion preventive line of paint along the waterline) and, most visibly of all, a new pair of landing platforms. These raised decks on either side of the wheelhouse restored the ship to her original appearance and greatly

assisted with embarkation at Southend Pier, although slightly reducing her passenger capacity to 235. Her programme was similar to the previous year, while John Megoran made great efforts to attract pre-booked coach parties and other charters as well as running promotional trips for local radio stations and ensuring that the ship was widely advertised. Sailings from Southend were adversely effected both by the weather and the fact that the pier was cut in two by a passing cargo ship and had to be closed for a short period. *Kingswear Castle* made no fewer than five trips to London, twice to Gravesend and on 7 June to Greenwich for the Thames Barge Match, on which occasion she broke new ground by steaming up the river to a point just above Cannon Street railway bridge. The fourth visit took place during a September charter when she met Waverley in the Pool of London, and the fifth in early October to Tilbury. It was also planned to take the ship across the Thames estuary to operate a series of cruises on the rivers

Kingswear Castle at Rochester Pier on the river Medway in 2001, with Rochester Castle behind. RODDY MCKEE

Blackwater and Colne from Maldon and Colchester respectively between 29 and 31 August but, sadly, strong wind warnings prevented the ship from leaving the Medway. As if to underline the magnificent work undertaken by the restoration team and crew in returning the ship to service, *Kingswear Castle* was named as winner of the maritime section of the British Coal Steam Heritage Award 1985-86 and was chosen as the venue for the presentations which took place on 5 July. The now traditional meetings with *Waverley* on the Medway and at Whitstable during September were supplemented by an extra meeting at Southend where passengers were enabled to change ships and sail on two paddlers in one day. A successful year was rounded off by two innovative Christmas cruises, complete with Santa Claus, during which the ship received her own, well deserved gift of a £3,000 cheque raised by members of the P.S.P.S. Wessex and London branches.

Over the next few years, *Kingswear Castle*'s business model was steadily refined in the light of experience, with more and more emphasis being placed on obtaining advance bookings from coach operators and other members of the travel and tourism trade. Behind the scenes John Megoran was proving to be a highly effective general manager and ambassador for the ship. During the winter months he spent endless hours publicising the ship at trade and travel fairs, contacting coach operators and potential charterers and ensuring that her clear and colourful annual programmes were available well in advance. This persistence paid off and revenue from pre-booked groups increased steadily. The programme of public sailings crystallised into a pattern of short afternoon and evening cruises from Chatham and Strood piers, interspersed with longer day trips to the Swale, Whitstable, Southend and elsewhere, as well as the annual Christmas cruises and meetings with Waverley and the P.S.P.S.'s newly acquired classic motor ship *Balmoral*. Always keen to add a little variety, John Megoran managed to take the ship to somewhere new nearly every season. In 1987 she ran a trip from Southend up Leigh Creek; introduced the 'Wharfs, Creeks and Jetties' cruise to the more remote corners of the Medway; called at Dartford International Freight Terminal and Chatham Sun Pier; and paid her first visit to the new London Bridge City Pier, which was to be her base on many subsequent visits to London. In 1988 she added special cheap Thursday trips during the school summer holidays; made a non-landing cruise from Whitstable to Herne Bay; and introduced an extremely popular series of 'Jazz Jamboree' sailings. 1989 saw the introduction of pre-booked cream teas; calls at a stone breakwater on Sheerness beach and the newly constructed pier at Rochester; a two day charter operating from Kingsnorth Power Station; a fascinating sail up Dam Head Creek to berth alongside the paddle steamer *Medway Queen*; and visits to *HMS Belfast* in the Pool of London.

Kingswear Castle also began to attract the attention of the media. In April 1987 the ship was steamed for the filming of a TV programme called *Highway* featuring Sir Harry Secombe. A further charter for 1 June 1987 did not at first excite any attention since it had been booked under a cover name. Only later did it emerge that Conservative Central Office was behind the event, and only when police frogmen began to examine

Alongside the paddle steamer *Medway Queen*. ASHLEY GILL

Sir Harry Secombe aboard for the TV programme *Highway*. STAFFORD ELLERMAN

Kingswear Castle as *Le Bonheur* in *Around the World in 80 Days*. STAFFORD ELLERMAN

the ship''s bottom and sniffer dogs appeared in her saloons did it become apparent that something was afoot! In the event it was the Prime Minister of the day, Margaret Thatcher, who embarked at Chatham as part of her election tour of the Medway towns and joined John Megoran in the wheelhouse as the steamer made her way to Gillingham. Then, in August 1988 the ship was fitted with a large temporary cabin on her foredeck and transformed into the French packet steamer *Le Bonheur* for the filming of *Around the World in 80 Days* starring Peter Ustinov, Robert Morley and Eric Idle. These were

to be the first of many high-profile appearances over the years ahead, amongst which were the BBC productions of *Our Mutual Friend* (1998); *Great Expectations* (1999); the popular archaeology series *Time Team*; Prince Edward's production of *Crown & Country*; Peter Ackroyd's *Thames: Sacred River* (2008); *Countryfile* (2009); and many more. From 1996 until 2000 the ship also played host to the *Mail on Sunday*'s Annual Poetry Prize judging panel chaired by the late Auberon Waugh.

Despite the steadily-rising revenue, the ship's continued

Pool of London with HMS *Birmingham* and HMS *Belfast*. P.S.P.S. ARCHIVE

Prime Minister Margaret Thatcher in 1987. P.S.P.S. ARCHIVE

Kingswear Castle passing Upnor Castle on the river Medway. Wooden shelters aft of the paddle boxes were fitted 1988-89. JOHN MEGORAN

operation was only possible because of her relatively low operating costs and the willingness of her small, permanent crew to take on a wide variety of tasks. In addition to taking the ship to sea each day, her master and manager John Megoran took on the full range of office functions - timetabling, marketing, banking, buying catering supplies and ship's gear, and ensuring compliance with the increasingly complex safety and maritime legislation. A rota of part time engineers ensured that the wonderful 1904 engine was in constant good order and carried out the winter maintenance programme. The crew was completed by two multi-purpose hands who handled the ropes, served refreshments, collected tickets and did anything else which was required. This small team was supported by the trustees and directors and a group of dedicated volunteers without whom the operation could not possibly have succeeded .

One particularly significant crew member from the start of operations until 2006 was Chris Smith. Having begun his involvement with the ship as a volunteer during the restoration phase he had an intimate knowledge of every inch of the ship's structure. After serving as a deck hand / purser / steward, he went on to obtain his boatmaster's licence and acted as regular relief master before moving below decks to serve as chief engineer for many years. During the winter months he was responsible for much of the improvement work on board. The first fruits of Chris's skills appeared during the winter of 1988-89 when he constructed wooden shelters beneath the landing platforms aft of each paddle box. Although some purists complained that these additions detracted from the ship's appearance, they definitely increased passenger comfort. Sliding doors placed athwartships cut down draughts and, combined with the traditional full awning and new optional side-screens, meant that the aft end of the upper deck could be completely enclosed during inclement weather, making it a far more suitable space for special events and evening cruises.

During 1992 the ship's owning company, Paddle Steam Navigation Ltd, was reconstituted as the Paddle Steamer Kingswear Castle Trust Ltd., to better reflect the charitable nature of the operation. Improvements to the fabric of the ship continued steadily throughout her time on the Medway. The announcement that new Department of Transport regulations regarding the survivability of passenger vessels would come into force by 1994 led to a major fund raising effort and by the start of the 1994 season *Kingswear Castle* had been made fully compliant by the provision of the required lifejackets, rafts, scrambling nets and additional bilge pumps. Her Class 6 passenger certificate was increased to 235 and she was now permitted to carry passengers across Sea Reach between the Medway and Southend. During the winter of 1993-94 the ship's bottom was also completely re-plated by the Crescent Shipyard, with generous financial help from Rochester City Council. During the following year, in order to increase the frequency of her sailings from Rochester Pier, *Kingswear Castle*'s funnel was modified to enabled it to be hinged down to pass under Rochester Bridge at high tide and her slender

Kingswear Castle's funnel hinged in 1995 to improve tidal navigation frequency of Rochester Bridge. RICHARD DE JONG

mast was divided to give a short topmast which could be housed or raised at will. To assist manoeuvrability a bow thrust unit was fitted, but was seldom used by John Megoran who generally preferred to use traditional methods of paddle steamer handling. The motor and hydraulics for the unit were subsequently removed. 1996 saw the ship appear with a larger engine room skylight which allowed passengers a far better view of the engines turning, while the white top strake around her hull disappeared and her boot topping returned to red.

The year 1999 marked *Kingswear Castle*'s 75th birthday and the timing was perfect to announce that the Heritage Lottery Fund had agreed to pay 80% towards the cost of a replacement boiler with the remaining 20% match funding being supplied by the P.S.P.S., the Manifold Trust and the Paddle Steamer Kingswear Castle Trust itself. After evaluating eight tenders, an order for the replacement boiler was placed with Wellman Robey Ltd. for delivery in January 2001. By the end of that month *Kingswear Castle* was on the Acorn Shipyard slipway at Strood and her 1962 boiler had been removed. While work was in hand on steel work repairs, cleaning and painting in the boiler space, the construction of a new hot-riveted 'fiddley' (the box over the boiler upon which

the funnel sits) was undertaken by Martin Staniforth and, when the new boiler arrived on 6 March, everything was ready for it to be lowered into the steamer immediately. While she was on the slip the steelwork and oak rubbing band of the starboard sponson had also been replaced and the final task in a truly momentous thirteen-week refit was the installation of a new, lightweight mast of the original height designed to be hinged forward to the horizontal for passage under Rochester Bridge.

Work to improve and maintain *Kingswear Castle* never ceased. Over the next thirteen years the port sponson, both paddle boxes and her forward coach roof were replaced, large areas of deck renewed, and replicas of her original etched glass saloon windows bearing an image of the eponymous *Kingswear Castle* were fitted. Although ideal for the calm waters of the Dart, *Kingswear Castle*'s forward well deck, from which steps led down into the saloon, was very close to the waterline and could prove a little vulnerable to boisterous weather or the wash of passing ships. Even modest amounts of water splashing over the bulwarks could result in wet saloon carpets and prove daunting for more elderly passengers wishing to go below in search of refreshments. Consequently, in the spring of 2005 the entrance to the saloon was sealed, the deck level in the forward well raised, self-draining scuppers fitted and an alternative companionway created, leading down

Steam being raised in *Kingswear Castle*'s new boiler. RODDY MCKEE

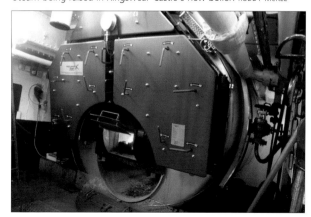

Aboard *Kingswear Castle* at Medway barge match in 2008, showing the new companionway to the forward saloon.

Kingswear Castle's programme and in 2000 she made a unique call at Waterloo Millennium Pier to land a charter party for a visit to the London Eye. The period 2002-2005 added trips from the Pool of London upriver to Putney, waters not plied by a paddle steamer for seventy years. However, operating conditions for *Kingswear Castle* in London had grown more difficult due largely to the success of the new high-speed river bus service which meant that overnight berths at central London piers were no longer available at an affordable price. Positioning runs to alternative moorings were long and extravagant on fuel, which could not be replenished until she got home to the Medway. Thus reluctantly it was decided that the 2005 London visit would be her last unless conditions changed again. 2005 also saw the unexpected and indefinite closure of Strood Pier due to safety reasons, following which all full day cruises commenced at Chatham.

During the 1990s the ship's income rose steadily year on year, peaking in 2006. Whilst the increased number of visitors to the Chatham Historic Dockyard led to a slight increase in passing trade, it was charters, coach parties and pre-booked tickets which continued to make up the bulk of her revenue assisted by the introduction of an award-winning website and on-line booking system. Wage bills had been reduced to an

to the saloon from the upper deck. During the winter of 2010-11 a new low pressure connecting rod was fitted to the main engine and major work undertaken on various of the ship's pumps.

Throughout the 1990s and the first decade of the new century the mainstay of *Kingswear Castle*'s public sailings were short afternoon cruises from The Historic Dockyard Chatham; Rochester Pier; and evening jazz cruises; together with a gradually evolving programme of full day trips to Southend; the Swale; Whitstable; the creeks and wharves of the Medway; also round the Isle of Sheppey; up river towards New Hythe, to view the annual Medway Barge Match; and to meet the *Waverley*. A series of innovative and popular 'Learn to operate a paddle steamer' courses were introduced and the season generally ended with a bird watching cruise to some of the less visited backwaters of the Medway.

An annual visit to London continued to feature in

Kingswear Castle's 1904 vintage, Cox & Co. of Falmouth built engine.
RICHARD DE JONG

absolute minimum by employing only the Master and Engineer on a full time basis plus some paid undergraduate staff in high season, with volunteers undertaking most of the crewing duties together with a substantial proportion of the winter maintenance. Falling interest rates, however, meant that the prudent cash reserves accumulated over the years were no longer accruing any significant interest and, with a run of seasons characterised by poor weather and recession causing a small fall in bookings, the Trust's mind was once again focussed on *Kingswear Castle*'s long term future. Even in the most buoyant of seasons the operation was financially marginal, and the ship's magnificent condition and outstanding reliability had been dependent on the herculean efforts of John Megoran supported by the engineers, trustees, an outstanding team of volunteers, and P.S.P.S. financial contributions to major projects. Although there was no crisis, there was a general awareness that the status quo could not be sustained indefinitely.

Meanwhile, down in Devon, the Dart Valley Railway had acquired the major passenger boat fleets on the river and in 2010 they merged these with their railway and bus operations to trade as the Dartmouth Steam Railway & Riverboat Company. The company offered a wide and imaginative range of excursions and its new management, realising how well an original, coal-fired Dart paddle steamer would fit into their operations, approached the Trust to discuss the possibility of *Kingswear Castle* making an extended visit to the Dart. Although the initial proposal proved impractical, the two organisations maintained friendly relations and, following further discussions, the prospect arose of *Kingswear Castle* returning to the Dart on long-term charter. After detailed negotiations the Trust felt able to recommend to the P.S.P.S. Council of Management that the proposed arrangement would be in the ship's best long-term interests provided the conditions of the agreement were right. There was a compelling logic and beauty in returning her to the river for which she was designed and affording her the comfort of once again becoming a member of a fleet. It was clear that the Dart company had the workshop facilities, slipways and steam

Kingswear Castle alongside Putney Pier, 5 May 2002.

engineering skills to maintain her to the high standards established on the Medway, as well as the customer base and marketing expertise to see her fully-employed.

Thus, as the 2012 season progressed and the final details of the charter agreement became the province of the lawyers for both parties. *Kingswear Castle*, looking as immaculate as ever, made the best of the dreadful summer weather. Her last timetabled sailing was a bird watching trip on 13 October, but her season was extended with a series of afternoon cruises during the school half-term holidays and a final Medway cruise on 28 October. Shortly after she had retreated to winter lay-up negotiations were finally concluded and it was announced that an agreement had been finalised for the ship to return to the Dart in 2013. Her remarkable 29 season career on the Medway was over. Needless to say, the news caused great sadness among the many organisations and individuals who had supported her over the years, and especially to the loyal and dedicated band of volunteers who had contributed so much to one of the most successful operational preservation projects in British maritime history. It is a testament to all concerned, and especially to her Master, John Megoran, that they were willing to deprive themselves of their much-loved ship in order to ensure her long term future.

Kingswear Castle leaving the river Medway for Dartmouth on 11 December 2012, under tow from the tug *Christine*. JOHN MEGORAN

HOME TO THE RIVER DART

The formal agreement to return *Kingswear Castle* to the river Dart was signed on 15 November 2012. The ship continued to be owned by the Paddle Steamer Kingswear Castle Trust Ltd. but was let on a 15 year long term charter to Dart Pleasure Craft Ltd, (D.P.C.) a wholly-owned subsidiary of the Dart Valley Railway PLC., both of whom trade as the Dartmouth Steam Railway & Riverboat Company.

Things then moved remarkably quickly. On 26 November steam was raised again and the ship paddled upstream to Acorn Shipyard at Rochester where her life rafts were put ashore. On her return to Thunderbolt Pier John Megoran indulged his love for handling the paddler by taking her out into the Medway one final time, running up and down at full power and sounding the whistle until almost every last pound of steam had been used up. It must have been a very emotional moment for a man who, having commanded the paddler for 27 years, is certainly one of the longest-serving paddle steamer captains in history and an undoubted expert in his art.

Kingswear Castle was formally delivered to D.P.C. at Chatham on 30 November, after which that company became fully responsible for her delivery and subsequent crewing, maintenance and operation on the Dart. Following a visit from a Maritime and Coastguard Agency (MCA) surveyor the ship was then made ready for towing. All windows and portholes were boarded up, a new deck plate with two special towing eyes was manufactured and inserted under the windlass, the paddle shaft was locked, the lower floats removed from the paddle wheels to reduce resistance, and the aft well deck had temporary bulwarks fitted to reduce the risk of waves coming on board. Once all necessary safety equipment for the voyage had been acquired and fitted, an MCA Load Line Exemption

Kingswear Castle en-route to Dartmouth on 18 December 2012, under tow off Portland Bill. BRIAN JACKSON

Kingswear Castle arrives in the mouth of the river Dart on 18 December 2012, greeted by her old fleet mate *Dartmouth Castle*. SANDI ARMSTRONG

Certificate was issued for the tow and the Medway-based tug *Christine* was placed on standby for a suitable period of high pressure and calm seas. The necessary break in the weather arrived on 11 December when *Christine*, under the command of her owner Alan Pratt, took *Kingswear Castle* away from Thunderbolt Pier for the last time at 0900 on their 250 mile journey. Once clear of the Medway good progress was made and by nightfall *Kingswear Castle* was passing Folkestone in a snow storm. Dawn on 12 December found her off Old Harry Rocks on the Dorset coast, but a steadily increasing wind led to a decision to put into Portland Harbour for shelter. Strong winds kept her alongside until 18 December when a temporary lull allowed her to set off again at 0830. She cleared the choppy waters off Portland Bill an hour later and enjoyed a smooth passage across Lyme Bay, arriving in the mouth of the river Dart in the dusk at 1545.

Three of the Dart passenger fleet with horns blaring and fire hoses playing went out to meet and escort her in. She arrived off Kingswear just as the village clock was striking 4 o'clock, to be greeted by a steam locomotive blowing its whistle in welcome and a large crowd of spectators on both sides of the river. After 45 years absence, *Kingswear Castle* was safely back on the river of her birth.

During the week beginning 20 January 2013 steam was raised and from the 23rd the ship began a series of steaming trials on the Dart. Her experienced Medway engineer Nigel

Kingswear Castle arrives in Dartmouth Harbour to a spontaneous greeting by harbour vessels' sirens and specators ashore. SANDI ARMSTRONG

Kingswear Castle's first return to Totnes on Thursday 7 February 2013, when she undertook navigational and berthing trials.
SANDI ARMSTRONG

Thomas was in charge of the engine room and John Megoran was on hand to train the Dartmouth skippers in the arcane skill of handling a paddle steamer. A successful trial trip was made to Totnes on 7 February following which the ship was placed on the slipway at her traditional maintenance base in Old Mill Creek for refit and repainting prior to her entry into public service.

Kingswear Castle canting at Totnes Steamer Quay for the first time since 1965. Using a stern rope to the shore and the flow of the river, the 113ft steamer was turned in the time honoured manner before departing downstream to Dartmouth. SANDI ARMSTRONG

The Dart company immediately announced an extensive programme of sailings which would keep the ship in regular service from Easter until November, consisting of up to four harbour cruises per day and high-season trips to Totnes when the tides are right. The latter can be taken as a return trip or as part of a 'Paddle Steamer Round Robin' travelling one way on the river and completing the circuit by bus and steam train.

Although fully integrated with the rest of the Dart company's fleet of motor vessels (including her ex-River Dart Steamboat Co. Ltd. fleet-mates *Dartmouth Castle* and *Cardiff Castle*), *Kingswear Castle* retains her distinctive colour scheme and is marketed as a very special part of Dartmouth's history. Her 'maiden voyage' was a sell-out celebratory homecoming charity cruise on Good Friday 29 March departing Dartmouth at 1030 for a circular trip down to the river mouth and upstream as far as Dittisham and Greenway Quay, with all income donated to the P.S.P.S. To add to the sense of occasion a 'Paddle Steamer Express' steam train ran from Paignton to connect with the sailing.

The sight and sound of this stunning and historically important little ship once again steaming up and down the beautiful river Dart has rightly caused great excitement both locally and nationally. The harmonious co-operation between her preservationist owners and Dart Pleasure Craft Ltd. would appear to be a model of good practice and foresight, heralding many more years of her successful operation.

The sell-out 'maiden voyage' of *Kingswear Castle* on a bitterly cold, but triumphant, Good Friday 29 March 2013.

Dartmouth Castle.

Cardiff Castle. DARTMOUTH RIVERBOATS

Dart Explorer.

Dartmouth Castle 1947
Built in 1948 by Philips of Dartmouth for the River Dart Steamboat Co. Ltd. Fleet sister of *Kingswear Castle* for twenty years during their earlier, original career on the river Dart.
279 passengers. Twin screw.
81 tg, 85ft / 26m long x 20ft / 6m wide.
National Register of Historic Vessels Certificate No 299.

Cardiff Castle 1964
Built in 1964 by Bolsons of Poole for the River Dart Steamboat Co. Ltd. Fleet sister of *Kingswear Castle* for four years during their earlier, original career on the river Dart.
400 passengers. Twin screw.
115 tg, 100ft / 30.5m long x 21ft / 6.4m wide.

Dart Venturer 1982
Built as *Plymouth Venturer* in 1982 by Mashfords of Cremyll for Plymouth Boat Cruises Ltd.
300 passengers. Twin screw. 94 tg, 83ft / 25m long.

Dartmouth Princess 1990
Built as *Devon Belle II* in 1990 at Torpoint for K. J. Bridge.
156 passengers. 60ft / 18.3m long.
Currently used on the Dartmouth – Kingswear ferry.

Dart Explorer 1991
Built as *Devonair Belle* in 1991 by Voyager Yachts, of Millbrook.
300 passengers. 150 tg, 85ft / 25.9m long.
Catamaran hull.

Kingswear Princess 1991
Built as *Twin Star II* in 1978 for R. G. Passenger Launches' Thames ferry service for Ford workers at Dagenham – a successor therefore of the *Greenway Castle* of 1937.
200 passengers. 27 tg, 63ft / 19.2m long.
Catamaran hull.
Currently used on the Dartmouth – Kingswear ferry.

Dittisham Princess 1995
Built in 1995 for G. H. Ridalls & Sons.
185 passengers. Twin screw. 70ft / 21.3m long.

STEAMERS OF THE RIVER DART (AND ASSOCIATED MOTOR VESSELS)

Name	Built	Acq.	Disp	Type	Tons gross	Length b.p.	Width	Depth	Builder	Engine
St George Steam Packet Company										
Paul Pry	1827	1832	1836 ?	Wood PS	31 tons net	-	-	-	Wm Radford, Hereford	
Dart Steam Navigation Company - Variously: Holdsworth, Fogwill, Hingston, Bulley, Petherbridge, Mortimore etc										
Dart	1836	1837	1841	Wood PS	59	66.5	14.2	8.2	Bell. North Shields	
Dartmouth	1856	1856	1863	Iron/wood PS	41.8	85.3	12	5.4	Scott Russell, Millwall	2 cyl. osc. 20 hp
Fogwill, Follet										
Violante	1839	1847?	1854	Wood PS	24	73	10	4.1	Limehouse, London	
Bulley and others										
Undine	1847	1847?	1864	Iron PS	38	89.5	9.4	6.9	Thames Ironworks	
Charles Seale-Hayne, Moody - 1856-1859										
Dartmouth Steam Packet Company Ltd - 1859-1877										
Dartmouth & Torbay Steam Packet Company - 1877-1904										
River Dart Steamboat Company (1904-1906) incorporated as **River Dart Steamboat Company Ltd** (1906-1975)										
River Dart Boat & Leisure Company Ltd - 1975										
Louisa	1856	1856	1868	Iron/wood PS	35.1	90.2	9.1	3.6	Deptford, London	10 hp
Mary	1851	1858	1859	Iron PS	30.5	95	9	5.3	Glasgow	
Pilot	1852	1858	1879	Wood PS	101	84.8	17.9	9.5	South Shields	Grasshopper engine
Newcomin	1864	1864	1884	Iron PS	47	108	12	3.7	Lewis & Stockwell	J. Watt 2 cyl. osc.
Eclair	1865	1865	1868	Iron PS	210	179.8	20.2	8.5	Kirkpatrick McIntyre	Two 120 hp
Guide	1869	1869	1877	Wood PS	85	100	19.5	9.2	Harvey, Hayle	Side lever 50 hp
Dartmouth	1856	1871	1881	Iron/wood PS	41.8	85.3	12	5.4	Scott Russell, Millwall	2 cyl. osc. 20 hp
Hauley	1877	1877	1898	Iron SS	32	61.6	13.6	6.9	Harvey, Hayle	2 cyl. comp. inv.
Nimble	1878	1879	1910	Wood SS	17.2	57.8	10.1	5.5	Brixham	10 hp
Berry Castle	1880	1880	1917	Iron PS	73.3	108	14.1	5.1	Polyblank, Kingswear	Two cyl. osc. 32 hp
Dart	1883	1883	1893	Steel SS	12.2	54.4	8.6	2.7	Davis, Abingdon	

Name	Built	Acq.	Disp	Type	Tons gross	Length b.p.	Width	Depth	Builder	Engine
Dartmouth Castle	1885	1885	1907	Steel PS	59.4	100	13	6.3	Harvey, Hayle	Two cyl. osc.
Glenalva (charter?)	1885	c1894		Wood SS	8	46.5	8.4	3.5	Philip, Dartmouth	Two cyl.
Totnes Castle	1896	1896	1912	Steel PS	50.9	79	13.3	6..2	Philip, Dartmouth	Two cyl, comp. diag.
Kingswear Castle	1904	1904	1924	Steel PS	85	107.6	15.1	5.0	Cox, Falmouth	Two cyl. comp. diag.
Dartmouth Castle	1907	1907	1947	Steel PS	71	100.4	14.6	5.3	Cox, Falmouth	Two cyl, comp. diag.
Compton Castle	1914	1914	1964	Steel PS	97	108	17.6	3	Cox, Falmouth	Two cyl, comp. diag.
Berry Castle	1922	1922	1947	Wood MV	38	60	13	4.7	Philip, Dartmouth	Paraffin/petrol
Dittisham Castle	1922	1922	1940	Wood MV	13	38.6	9.9	4	-	-
Totnes Castle	1923	1923	1963	Steel PS	91	108	17.6	3	Philip, Dartmouth	Two cyl, comp. diag.
Kingswear Castle	1924	1924	1967	Steel PS	94	108	17.6	3	Philip, Dartmouth	Two cyl comp. diag.
Clifton Castle	1927	1927	1942	Steel MV	67	70	19.1	4.8	Philip, Dartmouth	3 x Paraffin/petrol
Greenway Castle	1937	1937	1938/51	Wood MV	17	44.8	11.2	4.3	Ferris Bank, Dartmouth	Diesel
Seymour Castle	1938	1938	1972	Wood MV	37	60.0	14.8	5.2	Ferris Bank, Dartmouth	Diesel
Dartmouth Castle	1948	1948	1975	Steel MV	81	85	20.6	6.0	Philip, Dartmouth	Twin Gleniffer Diesel
Berry Castle	1949	1949	1972	Steel MV	50	67	16.5	5.5	Philip, Dartmouth	Twin Gleniffer Diesel
Conway Castle	1963	1963	1977	Steel MV	115	100	21	8.3	Philip, Dartmouth	Twin Gleniffer Diesel
Cardiff Castle	1964	1964	1977	Steel MV	115	100	21	8.3	Bolson, Poole	Twin Gleniffer Diesel

Kingswear - Dartmouth Railway Ferry (Railway company owned steamers operated 1864-1876 by Dartmouth Steam Packet Company Ltd)

Dartmouth & Torbay Railway - 1864-1872

South Devon Railway - 1872-1876

Great Western Railway - 1876

Name	Built	Acq.	Disp	Type	Tons gross	Length b.p.	Width	Depth	Builder	Engine
Perseverance		1864	1869	PS		50-60?				
Dolphin	1869	1869	1908	Iron PS	61	104.6	15.2	6.4	Harvey, Hayle	2 cyl. osc.
The Mew	1908	1908	1954	Steel SS	117	90.2	22.4	8.3	Cox, Falmouth	2 x two cyl. comp. diag.

Devon Star Steamboat Co. Ltd (Wholly controlled company of River Dart Steamboat Company Ltd. 1961-1964)

Name	Built	Acq.	Disp	Type	Tons gross	Length b.p.	Width	Depth	Builder	Engine
Torbay Prince	1947	1947	1967	Wood MV	91	81	19	-	Blackmore, Bideford	Diesel

comp. = compound. cyl. = cylinder. diag. = diagonal. inv. = inverted. osc. = oscillating.
b.p.= registered measurement between perpenduculars, i.e. from front of stem post to back of stern post on the waterline, for calculation of harbour dues etc.

DEDICATION

The crew of the *Kingswear Castle* after her final Medway sailing on 28 October 2012. Left to right: Nigel Thomas, David Lawrence, Jill Harvey, Roddy McKee, Gerry Abrahams, Tim Corthorn and Capt John Megoran.

John Megoran, Master of the *Kingswear Castle* for nearly thirty years

This book is dedicated to the many individuals whose hard work and determination has made the restoration, preservation and continued operation of *Kingswear Castle* a reality. They include: MASTER AND MANAGER: John Megoran. DEPUTY: Chris Smith. RELIEF MASTERS: Roger Bolton, Chris Bordas, John Gurton, Martin Lee, Kit Lee,Terry Lilley, Dan McMillan, Steve Michel, David Neill, Chris Smith, Colin Wright.

ENGINEERS: Alan Beavan, Ken Blacklock, Mike Burgess, Geoff Bootle, David Giddy, Bill Hedges, Chris Jones, Jim Nuttall, Jonathan Nuttall, Harry Quirk, Mike Simms, Chris Smith (1991-2006), Daniel Smith, Ivan Squires, Martin Staniforth, Nigel Thomas (2008 to date), Dave Toft, Roger Toft.

TRUSTEES & DIRECTORS SINCE THE SHIP RE-ENTERED SERVICE: Alan Beavan, William Blakeney, Malcolm Cockell, Stafford Ellerman, Jeremy Gold, Colin Harrison, Guy Hundy, Chris Jones, Nick Knight, Richard Martin, John Megoran, Roddy McKee, Alan Peake, Eileen Pritchard, Bill Prynne.

VOLUNTEERS, LONG-SERVING CREW AND OFFICE STAFF: David Abrahams, Gerry Abrahams, Joe Abrahams, Lawrie Beal, Rachel Beardsley, John Bevan, Howard Bird, June Bushell, Pat Bushell, Geoff Bootle, Tim Corthorn, Simon Eaglestone, Stafford Ellerman, Tom Ferris, Andrew Gladwell, Jeremy Gold, Neil Grayshon, David Green, George Harris, Terry Harries, Colin Harrison, Jill Harvey, Mike Hodges, Guy Hundy, Brenda Ingielewicz, Chris Jones, Joe Marshallsay, Nick Knight, Brian Lawrence, David Lawrence, Nicky Legg, Martin Longhurst, Maurice Marryat, Roddy McKee, Fred Montague, Wendy Montague, Daniel Oates, William Oates, Kirsty Orsbourn, Tudor Owen, Alan Peake, Malcolm Pole, Tim Rice, Mike Rogers, Heather Rooke, Margaret Russell, Caroline Salmon, Richard Saye, Margaret Scroggs, Mike Sims, Daniel Smith, Chris Smith, Jane Smith, Toby Smith, Jean Spells, Patrick Taylor, Pam Thomas, Bernie Thompson, Dave Toft, Roger Toft, Peter Trigg, Charles Turner, Richard Turner, Sue Waldmeyer, Peter Walker, Brian Waters, Diane Wegg, Chris Wharfe, Kim Winfield, Marie Wood.

To anyone we have inadvertently omitted from this list, we give our apologies and thanks.

Chris Smith at work on the paddle wheels

Sources & Acknowledgements

The authors first researched the history of *Kingswear Castle* and her earlier fleet sister steamers for their 1987 publication *Passenger Steamers of the River Dart & Kingsbridge Estuary*. Edited and updated these researches still form the basis of *Kingswear Castle*'s earlier story. The following sources and acknowledgements therefore combine credit for both volumes.

For their generous help the authors thank: Sandi Armstrong; Tony Beardsell; William Bennet, Custodian of the Totnes Museums Trust; Robert Chapman; Don Collinson of Kingswear; Bernard Cox; G. E. Devins, Secretary, Evans & Reid Investment Co. Ltd.; R. Dobson of Stoke Gabriel; Stafford Ellerman; Ashley Gill; Andrew Gladwell, P.S.P.S. Archivist; Jeremy Gold; John Goss; Graham Grimshaw; Brian Jackson; A. R. Kingdom; Graham Langmuir; Bob Martin of Totnes; A. M. C. McGinnity; Roddy McKee; John Megoran, Master and manager of the *Kingswear Castle*; John Millar; Eric Payne; J. S. Peach; Ken Saunders; Chris Simmonds; I. H. Smart of Dartington; Mike Tedstone; Bernie Thompson; A. H. Waite of Dartmouth Museum Association; T. E. Williams, Director, R.D.S.Co. Ltd; K. M. Wills, Managing Director of Philip & Sons Ltd.

Sources

Dartmouth Shipping Registers 1824-1898,
    Devon Record Office
Dartmouth Shipping Transactions 1865-1912,
    Devon Record Office
Companies House, Cardiff:
    River Dart Steamboat Co. Ltd. records

Newspapers and Journals

Exeter Flying Post
Western Daily Mercury
Western Morning News
Totnes Times
Totnes Weekly Times
Devon News
Paddle Wheels, Journal of the Paddle Steamer Preservation Society

Bibliography

Boyle, I.	*Boat Trips in Devon & Cornwall*, 2010. And simplonpc.co.uk, passenger ship website
Blackhurst, D.	*Philip & Son Ltd., Shipbuilders & Engineers,* 2001
Clammer, R and Kittridge, A	*Passenger Steamers of the River Dart & Kingsbridge Estuary*, 1987
Collinson, D.	*The Chronicles of Dartmouth, an historical yearly log, 1854-1954*, 2000
Coton, R. H.	'History of the River Dart Steamboat Co. Ltd's steamers', *Paddle Wheels* No 43, 1970
Cranford, R.	*Up & Down the Dart*
Dix, F. L.	*Royal River Highway*, 1985
Farr, G.	*Westcountry Passenger Steamers*, 1967
Hamer, G.	*Trip Out* (passenger vessel listings) 1977-1985
Hemery, E.	*Historic Dart*, 1982
Kittridge, A.	'Evolution of the Kingswear Castle', *Paddle Wheels* No 120, 1990
Langley, M. and Small, E.	*Rivers and Ferries of South West England*, 1984
Mosley, B.	*Shipping of the River Dart*, 1969
Potts, C. R.	*The Newton Abbot to Kingswear Railway (1844-1988)*, 1988
Roche, T. W. E.	*A Shipman's Tale*, 1971
Russell, P.	*Dartmouth*, 1950
Russell, P.	*The Good Town of Totnes*, 1963
Smart, I. H.	'The Dartmouth Harbour Papers, III The Ferries', *Maritime South West*, No 12, 1999